BE STILL

120 DEVOTIONS FOR A PEACEFUL HEART

B&H
PUBLISHING
NASHVILLE, TENNESSEE

Contents

INTRODUCTION

If you have decided to pick up this book, you are probably tired, overworked, or anxious about the future. You may have one too many things on your plate, a few too many responsibilities to handle. The world feels like it is spinning just a little too fast for you to keep up. The reality is that you are not alone. Thousands of people deal with the frustrations that come from a lack of peace. They turn to friends, to family, to self-help books, and countless other remedies that only seem to treat the symptoms temporarily. But at the end of the day, the source of ultimate peace comes from stillness before God. We can try to sleep off our problems, escape our responsibilities, or postpone work that requires attention. These, however, are only temporary remedies that can lead to larger issues down the road.

There needs to be an end to constant frustration. We need a break from unending anxiety. We need to know there is an end to lostness and hopelessness. We need hope for the future, peace for the present, and acceptance of the past. Some days, however, it can feel as if the order is almost too high to have stillness for the soul. And yet, timeless truths have been delivered to us for thousands of years. We hold onto the promises of Scripture. In God's Word, we discover truths that give us strength, that free us from anxiety and allow us to live with peace and faith.

In this longing for sufficient rest, we find the purpose of *Be Still*. In this devotional, the reader will find 120 reminders of God's goodness and how He displays His love for us in our everyday lives. Sometimes, our hearts will be shocked into stillness from the kindness of a stranger. We will pause from a good thought given by a good friend. We will ponder the wisdom shared by a mentor. We will stop and observe God's craftsmanship. This devotional's purpose is to remind you of those moments and to be still in the joy of experiencing them.

While reading this book, it should be understood that this is not an attempt to create dysfunction in one's work. There is no mention in this book of relinquishing responsibilities. The hope of *Be Still* is recognition. This book provides messages for opportunities that every person can take to quiet the mind and still the soul. We can find stillness in prayer when we acknowledge that it is just as important to listen as well as speak to God. We note the calm that comes from a morning spent in His Word. We discuss the quiet appreciation that comes from loved ones. We point to the speechless awe that follows the witness of God's creation. In *Be Still*, the reader is provided with lessons that point to the need for a perspective shift. The reader discovers the quiet joy that comes from taking note of all that God has done and continues to do in our lives.

You will discover lessons about doing good work, cherishing the responsibilities at home, an appreciation for God's creation, the importance of a kind word, the joy of shared wisdom, and the thanksgiving that comes from knowing God's love. *Be Still* will serve as a daily reminder of these things, and so much more. We hope that after a person reads this devotional, they can find a new way of living in stillness, discover a new way to live, and know there is little reason to be engulfed in frustration when we serve such a big God.

Do not be mistaken. This devotional does not pretend you can "pray away" all of the anxieties of this world. There is no reason to pretend this life is not a hard one to live. The peace we are discussing is not removing the problems that each of us deals with but a promise that we are not alone during these difficulties. The dilemmas we all face are going to come. It is a sad reality of this world, but the greater joy is that we serve a God who does not leave us alone. He displays His glory by working in and through countless aspects of our lives.

God provides wisdom to those who are willing to be still and listen for it. He displays His glory throughout creation to those who are willing to stop and lay witness to it, and He gives kindness through countless loving relationships He has provided for us. The problem is that many of us are too busy to notice. We glue ourselves to our devices. We worship the work that needs doing and ignore the God who needs praising.

In *Be Still*, we hope to lead the reader to understand that stillness is not an escape. It is not a shirking of one's responsibilities or ignorance of the tasks at hand. It is trusting in God and the reliance upon Him that gives His children peace beyond understanding. We can move forward knowing that His goodness and His love are active in our lives. We can rest knowing that He is in control. We can know that all His works point to the good, and we can live in the joy that the all-powerful, all-knowing, and all-loving Creator has a plan that involves us.

So, take on the challenge of reading this devotional and be reminded of the goodness of God. Know that this journey is one that will leave you noticing God's creation, appreciating the love of friends and family, recognizing the importance of seeking wisdom, and leaning on the faith in God's timing, sovereignty, and love. If you have picked up this book, you probably already know about these things, but are you aware of them? Are you aware of God's goodness, or are you too busy to notice? You may understand that you are supposed to *be still* before the Lord, but have you ever taken the time to do it?

Whether you start your day with this devotional, read it during your lunch break, or end the day with it on your nightstand, take the time to quiet your mind, put aside the distractions, and be reminded of the importance of stillness before God.

QUIET THE BUSTLE

*Rest in God alone, my soul, for
my hope comes from him.*

PSALM 62:5

We live in a world inundated with convenience. We can work from wherever we please; have dinner provided on our doorsteps; and the vast majority of us have supercomputers nestled in our pockets with access to emails, calendars, and documents that allow us to do various tasks with mere swipes of our fingertips. In a world surrounded by convenience, we almost forget how easy it is to be overtaken by it all; almost as if there is an expectation to take part in the busy rhythms of modern life. It is as if we have been swept up in a current of technological convenience.

And what do we do to combat this river? Our vacations, escapes, and restful moments all center around the notion of "unplugging." Even though we are surrounded by tools that arguably make our lives easier, our greatest shared desire is to remove them from our lives and only have that which is in front of us as our primary focus. Though this connectivity has helped in incredible ways in regards to our careers, our friendships, and our family relationships, a mountain of convenience is still a mountain.

We all understand at our core that we have an innate desire to rest. It is ironic that in this day and age, we are more often than not in need of separation from the tools and applications that were created to bring ease to our daily lives.

So, what does this all mean? Well, we no longer live in the days of clocking in and clocking out. We no longer live in a time where we can leave work at work and leave home at home. We live in an era where our lives at work and our lives at home are so intertwined that the only remedy to this entanglement is shutting off the only things that keep the two connected. Our phones, laptops, smartwatches, and Bluetooth devices all buzz, ping, ring, and chime to draw us back into the connected world—leaving us in a prison of constant communication. It is no longer rare to find someone that responds to an email or text at the dinner table or sends out information just before bed. For many, staying connected has become just as necessary as breathing.

We are not meant to live this way. We were not created to be in a constant state of work. The Bible reminds us of the importance and necessity of rest. So put down the phone. Shut off the notifications. The hustle can wait until the morning. For now, however, take time to rest in the Lord. Take time to be still in His presence and quiet the hustle and bustle.

LORD, I KNOW I HAVE NOT PUT YOU FIRST. I HAVE CONSTANTLY BEEN DRAWN TO WORKING MORE AND MORE THAN I PROBABLY SHOULD. LORD, BE WITH ME. QUIET MY SOUL, AND ALLOW ME TO FIND REST IN YOU. AMEN.

WORRYING FOR TOMORROW

*"Therefore don't worry about tomorrow,
because tomorrow will worry about itself.
Each day has enough trouble of its own."*

MATTHEW 6:34

Chances are, you are more than likely reading this at nighttime. The kids are already in bed. The lunches are ready for tomorrow. You have already folded the laundry, or at the very least, it is sitting in the basket. It is the time of night where everything quiets. Everything starts to still, and the quiet has come to stay. For many, it is the time of night when the desires of getting in bed and reading a book or watching a show have become commonplace. And yet, for some, it can become a mad rush to cram in as many chores as possible before they can hit the pillow and force their bodies to shut down for the evening. It is a sad reality for all too many.

There is an email that should have been sent earlier and slipped through the cracks. Maybe there was a text message that should have been sent days ago. For the students, an assignment that should have been completed is now due tomorrow and they are *this close* to being finished with it. I am not saying that these moments should be ignored and shouldn't be handled with some level of urgency, but the reality is that all too often these moments occur, and all too often we fall into the trap of taking care of them during moments where we should be resting.

We lose hours of sleep on assignments that can wait until the morning. We fatigue our bodies while performing tasks that can wait until the next day. Sometimes, we even risk our sanity with the overwhelming stress that does not have to be there in the first place. Face it, the obstacles to our rest are often self-made.

For many of us, the most important remedy to this is trust. We have to be able to trust that God will sustain us in the future. So many moments where we stay up late on assignments for work or school keep us from being able to seek rest. We do not trust that there will be enough time in the future. We do not trust that we will have the energy to take care of the obstacles in the morning. This is not how we are called to live. This, whether we would like to admit it or not, is living in fear.

Listen. Are there going to be moments where we have to stay up and get the job done? Yes. Are there going to be nights where we need to stay up with the kids to make sure they have finished their work? Of course. Does this mean we are to live in this attitude? No, never. We were not designed to constantly worry about tomorrow. We were not made to live in fear. We were called to trust in God. Rest in Him. And let the worries of tomorrow take care of themselves.

LORD, FORGIVE ME. THERE ARE TIMES I HAVE WORRIED TOO MUCH AND TRUSTED YOU TOO LITTLE. REMIND ME OF YOUR GOODNESS, AND ALLOW ME TO FIND REST IN YOU AND TRUST THAT YOU WILL BE WITH ME TOMORROW. AMEN.

WAITING
PATIENTLY

*The LORD is good to those who wait for
him, to the person who seeks him.*

LAMENTATIONS 3:25

What has happened to the virtue of patience? We live in a time when groceries are delivered to our front door in a matter of hours. A click of a mouse can have any item we can think of arrive at our home in as little as twenty-four hours. Even most restaurants offer a delivery option. If you live in the developed world, there is a strong possibility you do not need the virtue of patience. Every want and desire can be fulfilled relatively quickly with a click of a mouse or tap or swipe of a finger. So this leaves us with a few important questions. Do we still understand the meaning of patience? What does it mean to wait in a world without waiting? How does patience show itself in a world where waiting is something of the past?

Patience looks a little differently in the twenty-first century. Many assume they exhibit patience by not checking their phone every hour to check for likes and comments. Some may think they are titans of patience when they successfully wait for their meal longer than thirty minutes. Few may even celebrate not losing their cool over a package taking longer than expected to be delivered. Is this really patience, though? Patience, at one time, meant waiting weeks for a letter. Patience meant having to "get there when we get there" without any help from GPS. Whether we want to admit it or not, we could all use a bit of testing when it comes down to patience.

With all of this technological advancement, there is one who has never changed in the way that He works: God. In a world of easy-access, prayer and waiting on God have become more of a chore. We pray for fast healing, immediate answers, and signs from above to allow us to understand what to do as quickly as possible. This, however, is not the right way to live. Too much of this kind of behavior can lead to viewing God as a gumball machine that fulfills every wish and desire we could even imagine.

While God does take care of our needs as Christians, He does so in a way that glorifies Him. Will God provide for your needs? Yes. Is it going to fall from the sky the moment you say "Amen"? Not likely. God blesses those who are patient. He blesses those who seek Him. Are these blessings immediate? Sometimes, but the true gift of God is knowing Him, seeking Him, and trusting Him in all moments. A true understanding of God's gifts come with humility, trust, and above all, patience.

LORD, I ADMIT THAT THERE ARE TIMES THAT I HAVE NOT WANTED TO WAIT ON YOU. I HAVE WANTED YOU TO FULFILL MY NEEDS AND WANTS RIGHT WHEN I ASK FOR THEM. LORD, TEACH ME TO WAIT PATIENTLY AND SEEK YOU, FOR YOU ARE GOOD AND SUPPLY ALL MY NEEDS. AMEN.

4

RUNNING THE COURSE

Wait for the LORD; be strong, and let your heart be courageous. Wait for the LORD.

PSALM 27:14

There are few things as disheartening as an illness. Being sick is no fun for anyone. Some will try to point out the perks that come with being sick. You do not have to go to work. You get to take naps, and you get to wear what you would normally wear to bed, but all day. These perks, however, never seem to outweigh the fever, the aches, and the overall unpleasant feelings that come with sickness. For most, illness is something that we just want to get over with and move on so that we can get back to our daily lives.

In hopes to find a remedy, many of us will go to a doctor's office or walk-in clinic and discuss treatment for our ailments. We seek out a prescription that will get us back on track or at least on the road to recovery. There are some moments, however, when the doctor will say that the sickness is just going to have to "run its course." There are few sentences more deflating than that. And yet, so many Americans have heard those words when dealing with the novel coronavirus. When many sought out treatment, most were told to allow the illness to run its course.

It's a difficult thing to hear. Whether we want to admit it or not, some terrifying moments are formed by the unknown. When we are forced to take steps down a unfamiliar path, with no semblance of assistance to guide us down the path, it can lead to a season of apprehension, frustration, and fear.

The reality is that many of us are called to wait. Sometimes, the only right thing to do is wait on the Lord and be patient. This is not something many of us do well. It is difficult for us to wait, especially in moments of fear. When our mind wanders, and our fear gets the better of us, it is easy for us to fall into the temptation of weakness. I am not discussing physical weakness, of course. I am talking about the spiritual kind. We cannot fall for this temptation. We are called to walk with courage, trust God, and keep moving forward, even in the midst of the unknown.

LORD, I KNOW THERE HAVE BEEN MOMENTS WHERE THE UNKNOWN HAS HAD A HOLD ON MY HEART WHEN IT SHOULD NOT HAVE. THERE HAVE BEEN TIMES WHEN THE FEAR OF THE FUTURE HAS KEPT ME FROM TRUSTING AND FOLLOWING AFTER YOU. FORGIVE ME IN THESE MOMENTS. ALLOW ME TO TAKE STEPS FORWARD AND TRUST IN YOU. REMIND MY HEART TO BE COURAGEOUS, AND REMIND ME MORE AND MORE TO PUT MY TRUST IN YOU. AMEN.

ULTIMATE PROTECTION

For you, LORD, bless the righteous one; you surround him with favor like a shield.

PSALM 5:12

What words pop out at you when you read the verse above? Do you focus on "righteous"? Does "favor" catch your eye? Maybe "shield" sparks your interest. For me, I find the word "surround" to be something completely captivating. Think about it for a moment. Without the word *surround*, we miss such a tremendous weight to the blessing mentioned in the verse. Without the word "surround," the verse could seem a little one-sided.

Imagine, for a moment, a shield. Do you have it? Perhaps it is wooden or metal. Maybe it is light and covers your chest, or maybe it is long and heavy and covers the whole length of your body. Whatever the case may be, I am willing to bet you imagined the fatal flaw with all shields. They only cover one side of the body. If a warrior is outmaneuvered and attacked on the unprotected side, a shield does not provide much use. But this is not what the verse says.

The Bible tells us that God's shield surrounds us. The one who is found to be righteous in the eyes of the Lord is protected on all sides. We, as Christians, are surrounded by God's favor. This may not mean that we will be blessed monetarily, with success, or that we will even find all of our worldly desires met.

God may bless us with money, an extravagant home, or a great job, but these are trinkets compared to the true favor that is offered.

The hard truth is that this world is going to throw countless frustrations, obstacles, and ailments in our direction. Our nice job, good home, and wealth do not protect us on all sides. Only God is the one who can provide that kind of favor. It is so easy to forget that it can take some of the most insignificant things to destroy all that we cherish in this world. And yet, many of us who are found righteous in the eyes of the Lord are able to live a life that is filled with blessings. It may take a few moments to notice them, but many times, our blessings are not so much the things that we receive as much as they are the things we are protected from.

We can take all the time in the world to count all of the good things that God has given us each day, but let us not be too quick to overlook all that God has protected us from.

LORD, THANK YOU FOR THE FAVOR YOU HAVE SHOWN OVER MY LIFE. THERE ARE MANY MOMENTS I FORGET TO ACKNOWLEDGE THE MOMENTS WHERE YOUR FAVOR HAS SO CLEARLY BEEN SHOWN. REMIND ME DAILY THAT NOT ALL FAVOR COMES IN THE FORM OF GIFTS AND BLESSINGS THAT ARE PROVIDED FOR MY LIFE, BUT ARE ALSO SHOWN IN THE FORM OF PROTECTION FROM THINGS THAT MAY HARM ME. AMEN.

6

REST COMES FROM HARD WORK

God blessed the seventh day and declared it holy,
for on it he rested from all his work of creation.

GENESIS 2:3

Even though this is a devotional discussing the importance of being still, it is equally important to point out that stillness is a result. It is the effect, not the cause. Some are admittedly a little too accepting of rest. Some of us boast about our ability to nap and lounge. Some can even take on major rest when the work at hand is relatively minor. Whatever the case may be, it is important to know why God created rest.

When God created everything, He was not tired. That would suggest that God can fatigue and become worn down. This is not the case. Eternal beings do not fall prey to weariness. Instead, God's rest was a result of good work—God appreciated all that He had accomplished. This was not only because His creation was good but also because work had been done in the first place. God did not simply jump onto the next task; He paused and reflected, and in that He found rest.

In this busy world of ours, it is so easy for us to forget that resting is not simply a way for us to recharge our batteries. If that was all it was, then work would feel like a check box that we tic so that we can move onto the next thing. Instead, from work, we find an appreciation for the work that has been done. Maybe that spreadsheet may feel tiresome, but without it, the company does not operate as well as it should. Maybe those kids may be exhausting to teach, but the world will one day be thankful that they were taught. Whether we realize it or not, our work brings goodness into the world. It provides for the needs of others in some way, shape, or form that we cannot even begin to fathom.

It is because of this that rest is a necessity. It is not simply because we are tired from the work we have finished, but even more so it is because God has given us the ability to work in the first place and that this work is one that is good. Good rest comes from good work. And good work is one that should be followed with rest. Anything short misses the point of work.

So, take a break every now and again. Go get a glass of water, but remember, rest is something that comes from completed work. Rest, if done properly, can be a form of worship and thanksgiving by acknowledging that the work is complete and that the work, above all else, was good.

LORD, ALLOW ME TO APPRECIATE THE GOODNESS IN WORK. WHEN I FINISH A DAY OF WORK, ALLOW ME TO BE ABLE TO LOOK AT ALL I HAVE DONE AT THE END OF THE DAY AND RESPOND WITH REST AND THANKSGIVING. AMEN.

BEING MARTHA

But Martha was distracted by her many tasks,
and she came up and asked, "Lord, don't
you care that my sister has left me to serve
alone? So tell her to give me a hand." The
Lord answered her, "Martha, Martha, you are
worried and upset about many things."

LUKE 10:40–41

There is one in every community. You probably know this person well, and if not, maybe you are this individual. Marthas exist in every town, in every church, and every friend group. This person is one who is a worrier. It is a specific kind of worry. It is not one filled with fear over the future, nor is it the kind that dwells over the unknown. No, this specific kind of worry lives in the reality that something needs to be completed with urgency and must be perfect.

A Martha cleans the house in a panic but rarely expects guests. She signs up for duties that overstretch her, and she still finds a way to pick up more responsibilities. She is the person who will grieve over a mess of a home when the only flaw is a pillow that may be askew. She may even find herself taking part in something she does not care about but will still participate because she knows that it needs to be done. Though we would all agree that a perfectionist has admirable qualities, we do not enjoy the company of these people for more than a few hours at a time. Why is this? Well, perfectionists, though respectable, are more often than not rather grating individuals because there never seems to be a moment of satisfaction.

For the Martha in our verse for today, her obsession was ensuring that the home was up to the standard of Jesus. Preparing her home for Jesus would seem like a worthy goal, and most would respect this, but her flaw was not in the preparation. Her mistake was her unwillingness to accept that her house was as clean as it was going to get. Otherwise, she would miss out on spending time with Jesus.

It is an issue that so many of us face today. How many times have we heard of this desire to get one's life back on track before returning to Christ? Think about the moments when we have tried to ensure that our life was right before heading back to church. An old country pastor explained it best. Trying to get our lives right before we come to Christ is like trying to walk off an illness before going to the doctor. Sometimes it does not matter how many home remedies we try, there are some things that only the Lord of Hosts can cure.

The point is this. Whatever has your attention is not going to be perfect. It never will be. So, instead of trying to find perfection, why don't you give it to the only One who has ever known perfection?

LORD, I KNOW THERE ARE TIMES WHEN I HAVE TRIED TO ENSURE THAT EVERYTHING IS PERFECT BEFORE I TAKE MY NEXT STEP IN TRUSTING YOU. REMIND ME TO BE STILL IN YOUR PRESENCE AND KNOW THAT YOU WILL TAKE CARE OF MY IMPERFECTIONS. AMEN.

NAP TIME

*Carry one another's burdens; in this way
you will fulfill the law of Christ.*

GALATIANS 6:2

As a new mother, Ashley has learned the value of sleep. She fully understands that the nights of going to sleep around nine and waking up around seven are not going to return right away. Her husband, a worship pastor, has done everything he can to ensure that Ashley can get as much rest as possible. He's even picked up an extra job to ensure that she can stay home with the baby for as long as she likes.

Even with all that he is doing, however, Ashley still has not gotten a full night of sleep. Their newborn has been quite the active baby, not wanting to sleep for much longer than a few hours. Because of this, Ashley has started to build a bit of anxiety every afternoon. Her exhaustion creeps over her to the point where she is in tears when nap time finally comes. This nap time, however, would be different. Ashley's husband would be home this afternoon and offer to put the baby down for the nap so that she can get a few hours of sleep before he leaves for his night shift. When she accepts, she stumbles to the bedroom and sleeps.

When her husband finally leaves for the night shift, he wakes her up gently. After he departs, she finds herself in tears, realizing that the baby is still asleep, that the house is clean, and that their little boy is sleeping soundly in his crib. Next to the crib, she would find a note saying, "You've done a lot. Let me do a little. I'll see you in the morning."

Sometimes, the only obstacle to someone receiving a bit of rest is having something taken off her plate. For new mothers, that plate can seem too full some days. For new employees, an extra project can feel like a burden that is too heavy. Even though the message of this devotional is to be still, sometimes we will be called to help others be still. So, take note. Observe those around you. Do they seem a little overwhelmed? Could they use a bit of rest? If, so, take the hint. Take a bit off of their plate and help them rest. You may never realize how much they may need it.

LORD, I KNOW THERE HAVE BEEN TIMES WHEN I HAVE BEEN SO CONSUMED WITH FINDING MY OWN SENSE OF PEACE THAT I HAVE SOMETIMES OVERLOOKED THE NEEDS OF OTHERS. I PRAY THAT YOU WORK IN MY HEART TO MAKE ME MORE OBSERVANT OF THE NEEDS OF OTHERS. REMIND ME TO CARE FOR THOSE AROUND ME AND HELP OTHERS FIND REST. YOU HAVE TAUGHT ME THE IMPORTANCE OF BEING STILL, ALLOW ME TO HELP OTHERS UNDERSTAND THE IMPORTANCE OF DOING THE SAME. AMEN.

HE IS FAITHFUL

If we confess our sins, he is faithful and righteous to forgive us our sins and to cleanse us from all unrighteousness.

1 JOHN 1:9

For some believers, the most difficult thing in the world for them to accomplish is to feel settled and assured in their faith. And yet, so many wish that they could. The lingering question of whether or not a person is truly saved can create unrest in the hearts and minds of some Christians.

Ask any youth minister and they will more than likely tell you that there is at least one person every year that wonders whether or not they are actually a Christian. Sure, they may have said "the prayer," been baptized, or even been told by a pastor that they are, but there is still an unsettled feeling in the soul of the wanderer.

For most of these individuals, one of the greatest remedies to their tortured psyche is found in the Bible. Today's verse points to the reality of God's faithfulness—and His response to our crying out to Him. If we confess the things which we have done wrong, then God is faithful in not only forgiving us but also cleansing us. What a powerful word! To cleanse is to absolve, to purify, to purge, and to restore us to the way we were originally meant to be. God loves us so much that forgiveness for our sins is not enough. God loves us too much to simply give us a pat on the back and tell us that we are forgiven. He does so much more than that. His cleansing of us takes away the sin.

He wipes it from our record. He no longer allows the wrongdoing to be a part of our lives. That is the kind of love, grace, and power we are talking about when we are discussing the love of God.

Many Christians find it difficult to rest in the knowledge that God has forgiven them for their sins. The reality is that God has done so much more than just forgiveness. He has also cleansed. So, when we think on God's love, we have to understand that His faithfulness goes deeper than simple forgiveness. God has not only forgiven us for sins we have committed and will commit. God has loved us enough to wipe them away from our records. That is a love we can live in. It is a love in which we can find rest.

LORD, THANK YOU FOR FORGIVING ME OF MY SINS. I KNOW I DO NOT DESERVE IT. BUT THANK YOU EVEN MORE FOR LOVING ME ENOUGH TO WIPE AWAY THE SINS FROM MY LIFE, FOR CLEANSING ME OF MY UNRIGHTEOUSNESS AND MAKING ME HOLY IN YOUR SIGHT. REMIND ME EACH DAY OF THIS LOVE SO THAT I CAN CELEBRATE IT AND FIND REST IN IT. AMEN.

10

IT'S A GIFT

Therefore, a Sabbath rest remains for God's people.
For the person who has entered his rest has rested
from his own works, just as God did from his.

HEBREWS 4:9–10

One of the wisest things that Samuel had ever heard his grandmother say is that "every gift comes with a purpose." He would find ways to combat the logic from time to time, but he could never escape the truth of the statement. The sleeping bag he was given as a child would bring him warmth on countless camping trips. His bicycle gave him the ability to ride to various places around town, and his cell phone gave him the ability to keep in contact with friends and family. Whether he liked it or not, each gift he had been given so far came with a purpose.

It is because of this logic that one Sunday afternoon he thought he had finally outsmarted his grandmother. He had been told that the Sabbath was a gift from God. When he pressed his Sunday school teacher for understanding what the Sabbath was, his teacher told him that it was a day of rest. Excited with the answer, Samuel told his grandmother that rest has no purpose. According to his logic, all you do is sit around when you rest. What kind of purpose can be in that?

With an understanding smile, she mentioned this issue to her husband. He came up with an idea that would get his attention. He told him he would

23

pay him one hundred dollars for one day of work. Samuel excitedly agreed to the prospect and showed up on their front porch at the break of dawn ready to earn his wages for the day.

What Samuel soon learned, however, was that there was no end to work on a farm if one was willing to look for it. He started by feeding the animals at seven. After he finished that, he was directed to pull weeds from the garden. After this, he was pointed to pick up garbage that had blown onto their land. When he had finished picking up trash, it was lunch time, and he sat on the porch to enjoy his lunch. His grandfather, however, had other plans.

"What do you think you're doing young man?" his grandfather barked at him.

"I was taking a break . . ." Samuel responded.

"I thought there was no purpose in rest?" His grandfather chuckled. "Now go water the plants."

Realizing what had just happened, his head sank as he rounded the corner to water the plants. As he picked up the pitcher, he heard that back door creak open and found a soft smile and a waving hand drawing him into the kitchen. His grandmother had made a meal for him. Humbled, he looked up at her and thanked her. She simply patted his head and said, "Rest a while . . . it's my gift to you . . ."

LORD, THANK YOU FOR REST. REMIND ME OF ITS IMPORTANCE EACH DAY AND ALLOW ME TO TAKE IT WITH THANKSGIVING. LORD, FORGIVE ME FOR WORKING PAST MY LIMIT AND NOT ACKNOWLEDGING THAT REST COMES WITH A PURPOSE AND IT IS A GIFT YOU HAVE MADE FOR ME. AMEN.

THE WHEAT FIELD

But ask the animals, and they will instruct you;
ask the birds of the sky, and they will tell you.
Or speak to the earth, and it will instruct you;
let the fish of the sea inform you. Which of all
these does not know that the hand of the LORD
has done this? The life of every living thing is in
his hand, as well as the breath of all humanity.

JOB 12:7–10

Jonathan is a runner. He has been for quite some time now. He runs three miles every other day at a minimum and takes part in a long run that could stretch anywhere between eight and twenty miles. He participates in a marathon every six months to keep a competitive edge, but most of the time, his running serves as a way to take note of the surrounding scenery. He enjoys putting on a little music, keeping a rhythm that matches the beat, and observing all of the natural wonders that he may come across on his run.

On his short runs, he still finds a way to notice something new. It might be wildlife or a unique home. It could be a large tree or maybe a pond. Whatever the sight may be, there is always something captivating to notice. There is nothing, however, quite as breathtaking as his wheat field.

Admittedly, he knows fully that it is not his, but the sight is something that only a lucky few have been blessed enough to behold for themselves. During his routine three-mile run, there is a hill. It is steep, and for a quarter of a mile, it can feel like a never-ending crawl to get to the top. Even though it is a relatively short distance, only some of the most seasoned runners can run through this obstacle without stopping to catch their breath. Needless to say, Jonathan dealt with the frustration of stopping for air.

As he walked to the top of the hill, gasping for a satisfactory breath, he paused. With his hands on his knees, his peripheral vision caught a break in the trees and saw a valley. Filling this valley was what appeared to be acres of unending shades of yellow and amber. It was awe-inspiring, and even though Jonathan knew he would likely never run through this spot without stopping, he found solace in knowing that it would not be because of his lack of fitness, but rather it would be because something as beautiful as the sight before him deserves to be seen, even if it forces him to be still.

HEAVENLY FATHER, IN OUR DAILY LIVES IT IS SO EASY FOR US TO PASS BY THE BEAUTY YOU HAVE CREATED. THERE ARE SO MANY DIFFERENT INDICATORS OF YOUR CRAFTSMANSHIP ALL AROUND US, AND YET, WE STILL FIND A WAY TO WALK RIGHT PAST IT WITHOUT EVEN NOTICING. REMIND US OF THE BEAUTY YOU HAVE CREATED AND REMIND US TO STOP AND TAKE NOTE OF THE GOODNESS YOU HAVE MADE. AMEN.

THE SILENT
TREATMENT

**Whoever shows contempt for his neighbor lacks
sense, but a person with understanding keeps silent.**

PROVERBS 11:12

Kathy is a woman of simple tastes. She enjoys a good book. She likes to go to a nice restaurant once in a while, and she will always take you up on going for a stroll through the park, but the one thing that is most sacred to her is her morning ritual. She has a cup of coffee, reads the Word, and lets her Yorkie sit in her lap while she reads. She even takes moments to watch the sunrise as the sun peaks over the roofs of the other homes in her neighborhood. For her, mornings should be quiet. Her husband, however, inadvertently has a different perspective.

You see, as much as Kathy loves her morning ritual, she despises the way it starts. Her husband, the early bird, wakes up every morning, bumps into walls, drags his feet, slides chairs, clanks against bowls, and makes breakfast without a care in the world. For him, the day has started; there is no reason to ease into it, and this behavior is one of the greatest frustrations of his daily routine. Simply put, he does everything she does, just loudly.

It finally came to the point when Kathy walked into her kitchen after her husband and sat down with an obvious look of frustration on her face.

Perplexed, her husband asked her why she was upset. She responded that she did not enjoy waking up to his drum solos every morning.

Now, her husband is known to tend toward the dramatic. He decided that the next morning, and many following after that, he would be as silent as possible. He would not say a word unless she first spoke to him. He would delicately pick up his bowl and do his best to quietly pour his cereal.

What astounded him was that after the third day of this behavior, he discovered that his quiet time was becoming more meaningful. His meal was something he enjoyed more, no longer shoveling it down so that he could get started with his workday, and there was something different about the sunrise. It was no longer an indicator of time passing. It was no longer a signal that he should be on his way. Now, the sunrise was the promise of a new day. As light crept across the grass and eliminated the shadows, the rising sun became a joy to be celebrated.

By the end of the week, Kathy's husband noticed his smirking wife and asked what had her so smug. Kathy winked at her husband and said, "It's amazing what you notice when you're a little quieter."

LORD, I ADMIT THERE ARE TIMES WHEN I AM MOVING SO FAST THAT I MISS OUT ON YOUR GOODNESS. I ASK THAT YOU QUIET MY SOUL. GIVE ME MOMENTS OF PEACE WHERE I CAN SEE HOW GOOD YOU ARE IN MY LIFE. LORD, REMIND ME TO STILL MY SOUL, AND BLESS ME IN DISPLAYING YOUR CREATION BEFORE ME. AMEN.

LANDSCAPE PHOTOGRAPHY

He lets me lie down in green pastures;
he leads me beside quiet waters.

PSALM 23:2

Every photographer that is serious about his or her craft has become aware of the Fine Art Photography Award. There are twenty different categories for the award, but the one that is one of the most contested is the landscape category. Thousands of photographers enter the contest as a way to show off their skill and patience that comes from taking brilliant pictures of natural scenery. There are two types of winners of this award: those who familiarize themselves with the area enough to capture the perfect photo at the best time or those who are lucky enough to snap a shot of natural phenomena. Some of the best pictures are taken by those who have a little bit of both skill and luck.

One such photographer came in second place with what many have described as a loss by a technicality. There is a picture taken by a man who laid down in the snows of Banff, Canada, for over seventeen hours before finally capturing one of the best shots that has ever been appreciated by both the technical and artistic crowds in the photography community.

In the shot, a man captures the sunrise peeking over the mountains of the national park. The picture shows how the light has crept over the snows of unseasonably early winter. In telling the story, he mentions how he had laid in the snow overnight, capturing pictures of the northern lights and how the moonlight shone on the crystallized snow before him. He admits that he was after a night shot. He also shares how frustrating it was to have over three hundred shots of the night and turn in one of ten that he had captured in the morning. But for him, there was something special about the picture that he had captured.

In the photo, we see the sun. Its light is providing a sheen to the snowy landscape underneath it. But also in the picture, tucked in the back, is an arctic fox. Because winter had come so early, its coat had not changed yet. Its brownish blue fur contrasts its white surroundings, and it is caught looking playfully at the cameraman with his ear perked and head cocked to the side. It is almost as if he finds the photographer's presence as curious as his unchanging coat. The picture captures both the majesty of sunrise over wintry mountains and the whimsical nature of wildlife. When asked if he was disappointed in having spent so much time in the frigid wilderness, he said, "Of course not! Seventeen hours might seem like a waste of time to some, but I might not have ever captured this shot had I not been willing to be disciplined enough to be still and wait."

LORD, CHALLENGE ME TO BE STILL. GIVE ME OPPORTUNITIES TO REST AND ALLOW ME TO HAVE THE DISCIPLINE TO TRUST IN YOU AND WAIT FOR WHAT YOU WOULD SHOW ME. AMEN.

WOOD WORKING

*Whatever you do, do it from the heart, as
something done for the Lord and not for people.*

COLOSSIANS 3:23

Dr. Campbell has been a math professor for nearly thirty years. He holds two doctoral degrees in two forms of mathematics and has invented an equation that upper-level engineers have implemented in their work. He is one of the most respected minds in the field of mathematics. To this day, he teaches three seminars at a local college and has nearly four hundred students. He loves his work, but even he will admit to you that he is an incredibly busy man. Between grading papers, office hours, and tutoring his grandchildren, his mind tends to be dull by the end of the day. There is, however, something that he does to recharge his mental batteries: he works.

That feels a little strange to say. For Dr. Campbell, finding rest is found by working with his hands. Most of us would assume that finding rest and being still would be found in reading a good book, taking a nap, or even watching a show that takes minimal mental effort. This is not the case for Dr. Campbell. As the son of a carpenter, he remembers wisdom given to him at an early age. His father said, "Son, if you work with your mind, you should rest with your hands. If you work with your hands, you should rest with your mind."

Dr. Campbell remembers moments where his father would come home from his shop and read a book, play a game of chess, or even take time to learn a new skill. Dr. Campbell, being a man who works primarily with his mind, chooses to take the time to rest by working with his hands. His pastime is making wooden pens. He looks for fine wood and uses his tools to carve into the wood until they come out with a smooth finish and are ready to be given as gifts to his top ten students at the end of every semester. Attached to each pen is the word of wisdom to rest the mind by working with one's hands.

In this busy world, so many of us choose to rest in what, at first, may seem comfortable. If we work with our hands, it only seems natural for us to collapse into a chair and sleep until it is time to eat dinner. If we work with our minds, we assume that we should do something similar. This is not always the case. More often than not, the best forms of stillness and rest are found by doing something different. So, if your collar is blue, go home after a long day and read. If yours is white, maybe go out in the garage and tinker. Whatever you may choose, whatever part of your body that you work with, rest with the other. You may be surprised at the level of rest that comes from it.

LORD, THERE ARE SO MANY TIMES THAT I FEEL LIKE BEING STILL MUST ALWAYS BE LITERAL. ALLOW ME TO WORK HARD IN THE JOB OR RESPONSIBILITY THAT I HAVE, BUT ALSO REMIND ME THAT REST CAN SOMETIMES BE JUST TAKING A BREAK FROM WHAT I'M DOING AND CHOOSING TO DO SOMETHING DIFFERENT. AMEN.

15

RESTING IN WORSHIP

Is anyone among you suffering? He should pray.
Is anyone cheerful? He should sing praises.

JAMES 5:13

Jerry's father was a man of stoic behavior. Few ever remember him cracking jokes or telling stories. He was a no-nonsense gentleman. Do not misunderstand. He was caring, loving, generous, and would drop whatever he was doing to help his fellow man, but warm and fuzzy are not words that anyone would use to describe him. As others might say, he played everything a little close to the vest. Even though he was not exactly the warmest individual, he was a godly man and took his call to serve very seriously.

As a deacon, he was always one of the first to raise his hand to volunteer for a responsibility in the church. He was on the security team, the finance committee, the building team, and was even an advisor to the elders of the church when it came down to different kinds of church business. One of those responsibilities was accompanying his son to a youth conference.

At the conference, Jerry would see a side of his father that so rarely showed that he honestly did not know what to do when he saw it. He watched a flood of emotions overtake his father. During a contemporary worship service, Jerry watched his father cross his arms in near defiance of the new style of worship music. After the second song, he watched as his father's arms fell to his side, and by the fourth song, he watched his father's head bob to the music and watched as his body allowed him to sway from side to side. Jerry did not think much of it until the worship leader said that God had just put this song on his heart, and if his band would be willing, he would only play the piano to accompany this song. With the words "Be Thou My Vision," opening the song, Jerry watched as his father sat in his seat, and wept before the Lord.

Jerry did not know what to do, so he did what he had watched his father do so many times before. He put his hand on his father's shoulder, raised his hand to the sky, and worshiped until the end of the song.

The ride home was quiet. Jerry did not know what to say. The emotional man who had wept before him had disappeared and now, his hardened father had reappeared. To break the silence, Jerry finally asked, "Dad, are you okay? I've never seen that side of you in church." After a few more seconds of silence, his father said, "I just felt safe. I felt like I could let my guard down and worship the Lord."

So many times, we think that rest is something that can only come from working a long day. When sometimes, the most powerful forms of rest come from just being able to let down one's guard. Take heart in knowing that rest is being still before the Lord. Whether that means putting down a shovel or a shield does not change the stillness.

LORD, THANK YOU FOR GIVING ME REST. ALLOW ME TO BE ABLE TO TRUST IN YOU AND REMIND ME OF YOUR GOODNESS. REMIND ME THAT REST CAN BE LETTING DOWN MY GUARD AND REMIND ME OF THE LOVE YOU SHOW ME WHEN I PUT MY REST IN YOU. AMEN.

16

STOP SCROLLING

Set your minds on things above, not on earthly things.
COLOSSIANS 3:2

With the use of smartphones, more and more people are finding out that it is difficult to fall asleep. The constant strain on the eyes keeps people from being able to quiet the mind and fall asleep. Many doctors have blamed the level of blue light as the culprit for the lack of sleep in so many Americans. There are, however, a few psychologists who think it probably goes deeper than that. It is called the "treadmill effect."

Think about a treadmill for a second. The body does not work to propel itself forward as much as it tries to keep up with the belt. The same goes for scrolling for the mind. When running off of a treadmill, the body grows tired quicker than running on the treadmill. The reason is that the body not only has to keep moving with the pace, it also has to propel the body forward. When scrolling on one's phone, sleepy individuals are keeping their brains awake with a few swipes of one's thumb. They are not reading or thinking as much as they are having information poured into the mind.

In a way, our minds are keeping up with the digital belt of our phones—keeping our minds just tired enough to know we need to go to sleep, but just awake to scroll just a little more. Laying down before bed to read a book is one thing. It stills the mind. Praying with thanksgiving for the day the Lord has given you is a way to close the day with peace. Even taking the time to read God's

Word will be enough to bring one to a place of rest (especially if you start with Numbers). But in all seriousness, stillness and rest cannot be achieved by scrolling through post after post with a bright screen shining in one's face.

Rest is something that can only be found in the quiet. It is something that can only be found in the peaceful. Whether we want to admit it or not, rest will not come to a busy mind. It will not come to a mind that is being kept awake through digital distraction. So, put down the phone and pick up a book. Put away the social media and end your day with the Word of God. Or if you are up to it, instead of interacting with someone online, pray to the God who has loved you before time ever started. So, get off the mental treadmill, and go to God. You might be surprised at the rest and peace that comes from being near Him.

LORD, MY SOUL IS TIRED. I NEED TO REST. ALLOW ME TO FIND THAT REST IN YOU. REMIND ME OF YOUR GOODNESS AND ALLOW ME TO RESPOND WITH THANKSGIVING. HEAVENLY FATHER, REMIND ME TO PUT AWAY THE DISTRACTIONS OF THIS WORLD AND KEEP MY MIND ON YOU. ALLOW THIS SHIFT TO BRING ME PEACE AND REST. AMEN.

17

RUN THE RACE

Therefore, since we also have such a large cloud of witnesses surrounding us, let us lay aside every hindrance and the sin that so easily ensnares us. Let us run with endurance the race that lies before us.

HEBREWS 12:1

If you have ever talked to someone who runs long distances for their primary mode of exercise, they are quick to tell you that some of the best moments are when they hit a second wind. It is a moment that is difficult to explain, but essentially, there is a time in the middle of a long run where it just does not seem to be as challenging. Whatever the case may be, each step feels lighter. The pace is a bit faster, and the pavement feels just a little softer.

Endurance runners all over the world have experienced this to some degree. For some, it may last for a mile or two. For others, it could last the second half of the race. A second wind, however, is not something that runners keep in their back pocket for a race. It is not something to be relied upon. The greatest asset to a runner is the steadiness of one's heart. A runner must be able to keep his or her heart rate low. If it is too high, the runner will wear down too quickly and will not be able to finish the race. If it fluctuates too much, the body cannot keep a rhythm that allows them to continue for long distances. The goal is to find a pace that allows one's heart to keep a steady beat. Training the body to move quickly with a low heart rate is the key to success.

Regulating breathing and lowering one's heart rate is the best way to prepare for any upcoming race. A low heart rate, however, is not a possibility without any rest. Stillness is just as important to the runner's heart as is movement. A marathon runner cannot run to no end and expect to win a race without proper forms of rest. To be fair, no athlete can.

In life, I think we forget the importance of rest. Sometimes, we assume that the best way to run the race is by never stopping. We push through our jobs and take on the next project without a break. We take on responsibilities without looking at our tanks to see if they need refilling. We even jump to new opportunities without taking time to see if our batteries need recharging. Running the race is necessary. Endurance is key, but if our bodies and minds are weary, how adept will we be as runners with no rest? Run with vigor. Run to win, but do not forget. Resting is necessary for successful running.

LORD, I KNOW THERE ARE TIMES WHEN I AM SO FOCUSED ON MOVING FORWARD THAT I FORGET THE IMPORTANCE OF STOPPING TO CATCH MY BREATH. REMIND ME TO REST AND ALLOW ME TO ACCEPT THAT SOMETIMES EVEN THE FASTEST RUNNERS NEED TO STOP AND TAKE A BREAK FROM TIME TO TIME. AMEN.

18

TIME FOR BED

Start a youth out on his way; even when he grows old he will not depart from it.

PROVERBS 22:6

The greatest challenge on earth is finding a child who is ready for bed. Every step of the routine is a chore. When we say, "Let's change into our pajamas," they say, "Can I have just five more minutes?" When we tell them, "It's time to brush our teeth," they say, "I just want a quick glass of water." And when we say, "Okay, it's time for bed," they say, "Oops! I forgot to brush my teeth." Bedtime is one of the most challenging times to meet. Bedtime may be at 8:00, but I guarantee you that the majority of children find a way to make it to 8:05. And yet, we ensure our precocious negotiators get in bed with the lights out by a specific time. Why do we do this?

For many of us, the reason is for our sanity. The couple hours of peace are as imperative as making sure our children get enough rest, but our goal is just that. We are to make sure our kids know how important rest is. At the end of a long day, it is easy to want to catch up on the things we feel like we've missed. We want to watch one more episode. We feel the need to finish a chapter, or we might even want to catch up on chores so that we do not have to deal with them later. Whatever the case may be, we teach our children that the routine of rest is necessary.

We understand that there are going to be times when we have to stay up and burn the midnight oil. There are going to be moments when projects fall in our laps, and we have to work until morning. That is why routine rest is so important. The lesson we learn as children is that even though there are hiccups that cause us to stay awake, we know there is a time for rest. It is easy for us to forget this. We live in a culture where "just a little bit more" is engrained in our society. Even though this is acceptable on special occasions, this is not the norm.

Simply put, we are called to rest. From when we are children, we are taught that rest is so important, that it often comes with a specific time. So, whether it is time for a nap or time for bed, understand the importance that even rest has a necessary place in our schedules. It is something we are all called to do.

LORD, I KNOW THERE ARE TIMES WHEN I HAVE FORGOTTEN THE LESSONS I'VE LEARNED AS A CHILD. I KNOW THE IMPORTANCE OF MAKING TIME FOR REST. REMIND ME OF THAT IMPORTANCE AND ALLOW ME TO FIND THE TIME TO BE ABLE TO LAY DOWN, CLOSE MY EYES, AND REST. I KNOW IT IS SOMETHING YOU HAVE MADE FOR ME. AMEN.

THURSDAY
NIGHTS

There is nothing better for a person than
to eat, drink, and enjoy his work. I have
seen that even this is from God's hand.

ECCLESIASTES 2:24

Pat is a man of tradition. He knows that Sunday is for church and understands that holidays are for family. Pat is the kind of man who believes in the yearly family vacation and believes that every Saturday is for chores around the house. He is the kind of man who holds many things sacred. There are, however, few things as necessary to him as his Thursday nights. You see, Pat is a blue-collar guy. He uses phrases like "four-on and three-off." He works ten-hour shifts from five in the morning to four in the afternoon. Thursdays are his Fridays.

His team, because they have been there twenty-plus years, have three-day weekends, and to celebrate, the eight of them go to a local burger joint and enjoy a meal together as a way to celebrate the end of the week. It has become a necessary part of his week. The only Thursdays that he will miss are ones that fall on holidays. At first, the weekly burger was just an excuse to have a meal with good friends from work, and at first, Pat's wife was not exactly thrilled with the ritual. In time, however, it grew from just being a meal. The men started bringing their Bibles. They started praying for one another, and over the years, their camaraderie shifted to community.

The meal served as a way to celebrate the work that had been done. The conversation served as a way to foster relationships. Their relationships with the Lord served as a way to bring one another closer to knowing God. This Thursday tradition was no longer a way to enjoy a meal with the guys. It was a way to rest in fellowship with fellow believers.

There are times when we think the follow-up to stopping work is to cease moving. More often than not, recharging batteries can appear to be celebration, joy, and laughter. Celebrating the work one has done with people you have come to know through the job is one of the best ways to relax. To have the addition of knowing the Lord with these people only adds more to the celebration.

So, when we find the moments of celebration that come from a job well done, we should take them. Though we may be tired at the end of a long day, celebrating good work with people you love working with can lead to a rest that seems unparalleled. So, if you are up to it, take time to go out with your coworkers and enjoy a meal after a long week. You may be surprised at the kind of rest that celebration can bring.

LORD, THERE ARE MOMENTS WHEN I FORGET THE PEACE THAT CAN COME FROM A GOOD FRIEND. THERE ARE TIMES WHEN I FORGET THAT THE CELEBRATION OF GOOD WORK CAN BRING TREMENDOUS PEACE. ALLOW ME TO CELEBRATE A FINISHED WORK, AND GIVE ME MOMENTS TO ENJOY THESE MOMENTS WITH GOOD FRIENDS. AMEN.

CHASING CHECKS

Keep your life free from the love of money. Be satisfied with what you have, for he himself has said, "I will never leave you or abandon you."

HEBREWS 13:5

Chelsea is talented and entrepreneurial. She is the kind of person who knows a little bit about everything. Chelsea is quick to learn and charismatic. If the job requires a bit of ingenuity, she is not afraid of the task and often sees it as a good opportunity for a challenge. Chelsea is the definition of a jack-of-all-trades. She would not claim to be a master of anything. She just knows a little bit about everything. This quality makes her a valuable asset. She does, like all of us, have a bit of a character flaw. Her's is that this entrepreneurial spirit will often give her a little bit of tunnel vision when it comes down to earning an income.

She helps run a website for a couple of businesses. She is a substitute teacher. She finds a couple of weekend gigs and drives a car for a ride-sharing app on her phone. With all of these opportunities to make money, there are some months that she has made more than $5,000 just doing various odd jobs. All of this was working well until she met her husband. Before marriage, Chelsea could find ways to fit him into her schedule and go on dates as well as performing the same way she always had. When marriage was on the horizon, however, there started to be a couple of issues that popped up in premarital counseling.

They both took part in an exercise that discussed expectations. Chelsea had a long list, all pointing to her desire to provide an income for her potential family. Her husband, however, only had a few. The one that stung was that he asked that his wife only have one job.

This expectation was devastating. There were some months where Chelsea could claim to have as many as five jobs. She could not imagine only having one. She responded that they would not make enough money if she only worked one job. As a software developer, her husband looked at her with a bit of confusion. Finally, the pastor asked, "Chelsea, how much money is enough money?"

His question was one that she had never pondered. Was there an amount that would satisfy her? For the first time, she thought about what she was doing. She thought about her third cup of coffee at two in the afternoon. She thought about her fourth night of fewer than six hours of sleep. She noted that though she could keep going, she was often tired. Her pastor looked at her and said, "We lose a lot of rest when our only movement is chasing checks."

The love of money is a dangerous thing. It is good to have in one's bank account but looking at it as a life raft is something that will only lead to exhaustion and frustration.

LORD, FORGIVE ME. I KNOW THERE ARE TIMES WHEN THE PAYCHECK HAS BEEN THE ONLY WAY I FEEL SAFE. I KNOW THERE ARE TIMES WHEN I HAVE CHASED MONEY MORE THAN TRUSTING YOU. REMIND ME OF YOUR GOODNESS. ALLOW ME TO PUT MY TRUST IN YOU AND NOT WHAT IS IN MY WALLET. AMEN.

LEARNING THE HARD WAY

Every person goes through a tendency of learning lessons through poor experiences. From the lessons learned, we can all point to someone who may have tried to guide us from having to learn the hard teachings. It is astounding the amount of peace we lose from not listening to wise counsel.

As children, we were taught the importance of studying for upcoming assignments, and yet, all of us can recall a time when we crammed for a test the night before. As young adults, we know about the importance of budgeting, and still, many Americans can recall one time in their lives where they had to live off of peanut butter and jelly sandwiches to make ends meet. As adults, we recognize the counsel from our elders to save for retirement. Still, that is the primary concern for so many Americans who are in their late forties and above.

The point is, with the ignorance of wisdom, we lose the peace that comes from following it. So many of us walk paths that have already been traveled without asking those who know the directions. Almost like children, we feel the desire to learn on our own. Our pride does not allow us to listen to those who may know better. This pride is what causes us to fall as hard as we do. When we inevitably fail, there is not a worse feeling than knowing that the failure did not have to happen, that we could have avoided the struggle.

For many of us, we think the only way to gain wisdom is through experience. We assume that we could not possibly take on the knowledge of other people's experiences. It is difficult for us to accept, but no greater joy comes from knowing the right path to take before we have taken our first steps. When we are lost, no greater peace is known than from finding someone who knows the way. As much as we hate to admit it, the work seems a little easier when we already know how to do it.

So, when you do not know how to do something, or you are not sure the right way to take on a task, do not be afraid to lean on the wisdom of those who are above you. In work, it might mean going to your supervisor and asking what they want out of a project. In life, it might mean going to a trusted individual and asking how they would handle a situation. The situation is a simple one when we think about it. Would you rather waste hours of energy trying to figure something out, or ask someone how to do what you are seeking to do?

LORD, MY ARROGANCE HAS KEPT ME AWAKE AT NIGHT. BECAUSE OF IT, I HAVE LOST HOURS OF REST THAT I COULD HAVE GAINED IF I ASKED FOR WISDOM. ALLOW ME TO SWALLOW MY PRIDE AND ASK OTHERS FOR HELP. DRIVE ME TO SEEK COUNSEL IN THE MOMENTS WHEN I AM UNSURE OF WHAT TO DO. AMEN.

GETTING IN OUR OWN WAY

In vain you get up early and stay up late,
working hard to have enough food—yes,
he gives sleep to the one he loves.

PSALM 127:2

No one is ever surprised that they are tired. Have you ever thought about that? Other than sickness, we are rarely shocked at the reasoning for our fatigue. At the end of a long day, when we note our tiredness, we always know why. Maybe we juggled too many plates. Maybe there was one project that was almost too much to handle. We may not want to admit this last one, but possibly our precious angels were acting more like unruly heathens. Whatever it is, when our heads hit the pillows with force, we always know why. Sadly, however, there are moments when our exhaustion was caused by our own doing.

When it comes down to taking on too many responsibilities, we often realize that we did not have to do this in the first place. This could be because we saw an opportunity we wanted to take on even though our plate was already filled with other responsibilities. Or worse, maybe our desire to please others is so great that we are willing to work to exhaustion for the sake of others' approval.

Sometimes it could just be one task that is so great that by the end of it, all we can do is collapse. Did we take this on knowing we were not equipped to take it on well? Or were we so arrogant that we assumed we would figure out how to do something we have never attempted? Our pride can often be the culprit of our exhaustion. And what of our rascals? What do we do when our castle is marked by chaos? Was letting them stay up that good of an idea? Did they need the extra dose of sugar? Our sweet babies can switch to near criminal behaviors if we indulge them too much.

The point is that you might be reading this with heavy eyelids that did not have to be as heavy as they are. You could have communicated that you had a little too much on your plate. You could have taken the time to ask for a bit of help, and you could have done something to keep the peace at home. This is not to say that the unpredictable never happens. We all know there are times when life is going to throw us a few curveballs. But if we are honest with ourselves, there have been times that we have gotten in our own way from having the rest we so desperately need.

LORD, I KNOW THERE ARE TIMES WHEN I HAVE MISSED OUT ON THE REST I NEED BECAUSE OF MY OWN DOING. DRIVE ME TO BE ABLE TO SAY NO TO UNNEEDED RESPONSIBILITIES, TO BE ABLE TO ASK FOR HELP WHEN I NEED IT, AND TO BE ABLE TO HANDLE THE MOMENTS OF CHAOS AS THEY COME. GIVE ME PEACE IN THE UNPREDICTABLE MOMENTS AND GIVE ME WISDOM IN THE MOMENTS THAT REQUIRE IT. AMEN.

COMFY CLOTHES

*May your faithful love comfort me as
you promised your servant.*

PSALM 119:76

As a mother of young boys, Heather has learned the importance of code phrases. She knows how imperative it is to communicate with her children what she wants to be done without giving away any ulterior motives. For instance, she rarely has to say, "Wash your hands." She only has to remind them that it is "time for dinner." She does not have to say, "Leave me alone." She says, "Why don't you boys go play outside?" And for her most clever phrase, she never says, "Get ready for bed." She only says, "Why don't we get into our comfy clothes." Then the three of them cuddle on the couch and watch a television show that will not get them riled up.

There is a secret to rest that everyone knows but rarely take the time to ponder. Rest is never discovered unless comfort is found first. For Heather, she understands that rest is avoided by little boys. They do their best to fight sleep as best they can. It is no wonder that nap time is often found wherever they collapse. It is because of this that Heather makes sure that her boys are comfortable before she puts them to bed. She has them brush their teeth. She turns the lights down low. She has them change into their "comfy clothes." And whenever the time for bed finally comes, the boys are prepared. They have found comfort, and even though they may grumble, they know they are ready for bed.

We have not changed as adults either. Whether we want to admit it or not, we fight opportunities to rest. There is always something else that we could be doing. We want to squeeze out just a few more moments of energy before we inevitably collapse. As much as we want to do anything and everything, we are not wired this way. We cannot simply go and go and go and then finally stop. There has to be an easing into our rest. Just as hearts need to prepare for worship, our bodies, minds, and souls need to prepare for rest.

So, how do we do this? How do we prepare for rest? What are our "comfy clothes"? Well, it starts with the mind. Dumping unneeded excitement into our brains is not going to help matters. Quiet the mind so that it is ready to shut down for the day. Next, it starts with our bodies, raised heart rates keep our bodies going. So, relax. Allow your body to find ease at the end of the day. And finally, the soul needs to be placed in that which brings rest. End your day with prayer and find that rest in God is unlike any that the world can bring.

LORD, I ADMIT I AM NOT VERY GOOD AT PREPARING TO BE STILL. I KEEP MY BODY GOING FOR AS LONG AS I CAN UNTIL I INEVITABLY LAND WHEREVER I FALL. ALLOW ME TO BE ABLE TO FIND REST IN YOU, AND GUIDE ME TO A STATE OF STILLNESS. AMEN.

GIVING REST TO THE WEARY

**No one is to seek his own good, but
the good of the other person.**

1 CORINTHIANS 10:24

Everyone takes part in a ministry of which they take ownership. They may not be the head of the ministry, but they have taken their service seriously. Greg does this for "Room in the Inn." Every Sunday afternoon, he arrives at the church, lays out twenty cots, places sheets on twenty mattresses, and even leaves a piece of chocolate and a mint next to the pillow of every bed. He then unlocks a closet that is filled with clothes and ensures that there is enough inventory for the men to be able to have three items from the closet. And finally, he contacts whichever Sunday school class is in charge of providing the meal for the night to double-check that everything will arrive in time for the men.

When the bus arrives, he greets the men, shares a meal with them, and spends the night on the couch as the men shower, find new clothes, and lay down for the evening. Then, in the morning, he sneaks off to a local fast-food restaurant and buys enough breakfast sandwiches for each man to leave with two. He is a giving man, and even though the night itself is one that is not filled with rest, there is nothing quite like the rest that comes from the Monday after serving all day Sunday. When he finally takes the time to rest that Monday morning, he does so with incredible ease because there is not a peace quite like the one that comes from giving to others the day before.

When asked if he is ever tired from doing this every Sunday night, he remarks, "Some of these men go without a place to sleep multiple nights a week. It only seems fair that I miss out on a little to be able to give that to others." A giving spirit is one that is overlooked when we think about the upcoming rest. We all know a generous person who burns out. But for every person who has been burned by fickle generosity, we know someone who finds their rest in providing it for others.

God has called us all to look out for our fellow man. We are to seek the good for others. Does that mean there will be moments where we are a little inconvenienced? Yes, but that does not mean that the peace that follows will not be worth it. So go out, serve a few people, and discover the blessings and peace that come from giving much to those who could only give a little.

HEAVENLY FATHER, THANK YOU FOR THE GENEROSITY THAT HAS BEEN SHOWN TO ME THROUGHOUT MY LIFE. EVERY INSTANCE HAS BEEN SOMETHING THAT HAS GIVEN ME BOTH PEACE AND JOY. REMIND ME OF THE IMPORTANCE TO SHOW THIS GENEROSITY TO OTHERS. ALLOW ME TO REACH OUT TO THOSE IN NEED AND CARE FOR THOSE AROUND ME. DRIVE ME TO GIVE REST TO THOSE WHO NEED IT. AMEN.

25

MOM'S WAKE-UP CALL

To slander no one, to avoid fighting, and to be kind, always showing gentleness to all people.

TITUS 3:2

On weekdays, it is not uncharacteristic for Taylor's father to wake him with a shout from downstairs. He has a habit of yelling, "You'll miss the bus!" almost every other morning. Taylor is not an irresponsible young man, nor is he one marked with defiance. He is just a teenager who is not what one would call a morning person. He is sluggish; he bumps into walls, and full consciousness is not something that greets him until the first bell to get to class. Saturdays, however, are a very different story.

On Saturday, he is not rebuked by his father's voice. There are no orders barked at him. Instead, he awakes from the soft tousle of his hairs from his mother. She rubs the strands playfully as a way to wake up her teenager the way she always has since he was a young boy. At that moment, he will shift his head this way and that as a way to beg for five more minutes of sleep, but his mother rarely gives them to him. Instead, she still plays with the curls of her boy's head and then gives a few pats on the top of his head before saying, "Your father will come next if you don't wake up . . ."

The hollow threat brings him to his feet, but it is his mother's gentleness that causes him to stir. In stillness and peace, we sometimes forget that there are moments when the rest must end. It is a frustrating place to be, but it happens to all of us. This ending, however, does not have to be abrupt. It does not have to be one that disappears in an instant. Just as we need to be lulled into rest, we cannot be shoved into awareness.

Many times, most of us think that an abrupt nature gets things accomplished. We hope to lie down and fall asleep when we have not prepared ourselves with gentleness to do so. The alarm buzzer goes off, and even though we hate it, we desperately wish we were the kind of person who can wake up. The reality is that these kinds of people who can shut off at night or awaken with alertness are few and far between. Just as a gentle nature is needed to find rest, a gentle push is necessary to wake. Gentleness, whether we realize it or not, is the key to a spirit that can live peacefully, whether still or moving.

LORD, I KNOW THERE HAVE BEEN TIMES WHEN I HAVE TRIED TO FORCE MYSELF TO REST OR WILL MYSELF TO START THE DAY. AND EVEN THOUGH THERE ARE TIMES WHEN THAT IS NECESSARY, I HAVE HELD ONTO THIS WAY OF LIVING MORE OFTEN THAN I SHOULD. REMIND ME THAT GENTLENESS IS JUST AS IMPORTANT AS DETERMINATION. ALLOW ME TO FIND REST AND AWAKEN FROM IT WITH A GENTLE SPIRIT. AMEN.

THE PEACEMAKER

*"Blessed are the peacemakers, for they
will be called sons of God."*

MATTHEW 5:9

In just about every church congregation, one will find at least one individual marked with a gentle spirit. They are not pushovers nor are they people who avoid confrontation. They are the ones who you would want to have nearby in a frustrating encounter. For one particular church in rural Mississippi, there is a deacon by the name of Floyd. He is a soft-spoken man and is not known to stir the pot in business meetings, Sunday school classes, or other church functions. He is famous for his kindness, but his greatest attribute as a deacon is not his willingness to serve or his business sense. Instead, people appreciate him most for his ability to diffuse tense situations. His pastor has even remarked that Floyd has a way of "stilling angry hearts."

You see, Floyd is a peacemaker. He is well-known for it. Even when people are angry, when Floyd is approaching, they almost become more frustrated because they expect to leave that conversation not as wrathful as they were. They all claim to fall under Floyd's "spell." Floyd's words, however, are not magic. There is no incantation that he sneaks into the conversation. His secret is a simple one. He listens and responds with gentleness. He hears out their frustrations, asks them how they arrived at this angry nature, and then offers a soft word for how to handle their anger. It is an easy formula to follow.

In this world, with social media, politics, and strained friendships, it is easy to identify the contrived nature of humanity. We, as much as we claim to hate it, like to fight. We find natural ease in our disdain for those with whom we disagree. And yet, men like Floyd thrive in days such as these. We need more Floyds in the world. We need more people who can cool the hot head, who can soften the stone heart, and who can still the restless spirit. In a world marked by chaos, it seems more and more apparent that the flames of our hearts need to be cooled by the gentleness of a soft word from peacemakers.

We are not always going to get along. We are guaranteed to find agreement, but the greatest fear of many peacemakers is that we will reach a place where people do not care about the hearts of their fellow men but will, instead, only care about being the one who is correct in their minds. It is okay to disagree from time to time. Human nature provides just enough nuance for us to never find complete agreement with others. That, however, cannot be the reason we cannot find joy and love for others and treat them with gentleness and kindness.

HEAVENLY FATHER, I ADMIT I HAVE NOT BEEN
A PEACEMAKER. THERE ARE TIMES WHEN
I CARE MORE ABOUT BEING RIGHT THAN
LOVING OTHERS. REMIND ME TO HAVE A
GENTLE SPIRIT TO THOSE WITH WHOM I FIND
CONFLICT. ALLOW MY HEART TO BE STILLED
BY THE PEACEMAKERS, AND ALLOW ME TO BE A
PEACEMAKER TO SHOW LOVE TO OTHERS. AMEN.

27

THE WILDFIRE OF ANGER

A gentle answer turns away anger, but
a harsh word stirs up wrath.

PROVERBS 15:1

It would be silly to ask if you have ever been angry. Of course, you have! We all have been there. Something causes our hearts to stir negatively. Someone may have wronged us. Someone said something about us that was not true, or someone has insulted us with their words or their behavior. Whatever the case may be, we have all been angry more times than we care to count. The worst part about anger, however, is that it is very contagious. Wrath, like a wildfire, can spread and destroy anything in its path. But there is one thing that can stop the heat of anger: the cooling touch of a loving word.

In the state of California, wildfires are almost a yearly occurrence. Some may argue that the causes come from climate change or poor forest management, but one thing that both parties acknowledge is that putting out these fires requires an outside source. Without helicopters dropping large amounts of water and flame retardants, the fires will burn and burn until there is nothing left. It is often the same for us. When the burning chaos of anger strikes our souls, we will likely burn until there is nothing left—leaving us depleted and alone. More often than not, our hearts need cooling from the kindness of others.

A forest fire, however, does not have to be the state of our hearts. Like the parks burned to the ground, there is almost always a discussion about how it would not have had to happen had it been smothered when it was just a spark. Had the fire not been left to burn or had the fire been put out when it was just a small flame, there would not have been the destruction that often occurs.

Sometimes we are so determined to get in the last word. People want so badly to have the right response that will put their opponent in their place. This, however, is not a godly life. It is not a life that is marked by the love of Christ. We have been called to turn away anger with gentleness, not stir it up with harshness. So, when the heat rises from those we may have hurt, when we see the spark shoot from their heart and witness anger and frustration start to build, respond with love. When wrath is building, respond with a gentle spirit and a loving word.

HEAVENLY FATHER, AS MUCH AS I DO NOT WANT TO ADMIT IT, I KNOW THERE ARE TIMES WHEN MY HEART CANNOT BE STILL BECAUSE OF MY ANGER. I KNOW THERE ARE TIMES WHEN I CANNOT FIND A CALM ATTITUDE BECAUSE OF THE WRATH IN MY SPIRIT. ALLOW ME TO LET IT GO. SOFTEN MY HEART WITH A LOVING WORD FROM OTHERS. ALLOW ME TO FIND GRACE FOR THOSE WHO HAVE WRONGED ME. AND ALLOW ME TO SEEK YOU IN TIMES WHEN I WISH TO SEEK MOMENTARY VENGEANCE. CALM THE FIRE IN ME, LORD, AND REMIND ME TO FOLLOW YOU. AMEN.

28

A CALM DEFENSE

**A fool gives full vent to his anger, but
a wise person holds it in check.**

PROVERBS 29:11

In high school, Mark was the kind of person you did not want to pick a fight with. He was not a person built like a fighter, nor was he a person who knew how to fight, but he was a force to be reckoned with. He was someone with whom you should not trifle. This respect was because of his attitude. He was not threatening, nor was he a bully. But instead, he remained calm. There was a stillness to him that was unshaken, and it helped that he tried to be friends with anyone. Do not get me wrong. It was high school. Many tried to ruffle his feathers, none succeeded. He respected those around him and paid no mind to those who sought to anger him.

This behavior followed him to his university where he would have his greatest challenge as a young Christian man: his philosophy professor. You see, this professor was an atheist, a militant one. At the beginning of every year, he would say, "If you're a Christian, you are not going to like me." It was an open challenge to those who would try and defy his atheistic notions. Mark, however, raised his hand and said, "Professor, as a Christian, are you going to mark me down if I try to like you?" His response earned a few chuckles and the ire of his professor. Over the semester, the two would openly debate concepts regarding ethics as well as the existence of God. The professor would win most of the debates, but Mark would always respond the same way, "It seems that you have stumped me for today." He would then smile, gather his things, and go to his next class after dismissal.

At the end of the semester, his professor stopped him and asked how he could still believe after losing every debate. His response was something that many of us can learn from today. "I'm an English major. I read many books, but if there is one thing I have learned, it is this: you are going to find what you look for. You *look* for ways to prove that God does not exist and I am *shown* every day that not only does He exist, but that He is alive and well. I respect you, professor. You sharpened me in ways that you will never know." The professor smirked at his response and said, "You will get an A in this class. Not because I agree with your stances, but because I agree with the poise in which you presented them. Most Christians waver, or present their defense with anger. You, however, were kind in your delivery. I rarely see that."

LORD, THANK YOU FOR BEING SO REAL IN MY LIFE. THANK YOU FOR REVEALING YOUR GOODNESS IN COUNTLESS WAYS. LORD, I PRAY FOR THOSE WHO DO NOT KNOW YOU. I PRAY FOR THOSE WHO ARE AGAINST YOU, AND I PRAY THAT YOU WILL GIVE ME A STILL HEART WHEN I ENCOUNTER THEM. REMIND ME TO LOVE THEM AND THAT THE GREATEST REFLECTION OF YOUR LOVE CAN BE SEEN IN THE WAY I LOVE THOSE WHO DO NOT KNOW YOU. AMEN.

LOVING THE ENEMY

**Bless those who persecute you;
bless and do not curse.**

ROMANS 12:14

No one likes a bully. All of us can identify a bully when we see one. They seek out those who they can harass with little worry of any retaliation. They look for the ones they assume are either weak physically or do not seem to have the backbone to stand up for themselves. Most of us can recall them in school, but the sad reality is that some of us may deal with them in our adult lives. Maybe they are in the form of a bad neighbor, or perhaps they exist as a micro-manager at work. They might even be a relative who never grew out of their role of picking on another family member. Whatever the case may be, every bully has familiar kryptonite: kindness.

Most bullies do not know what to do in the face of kindness. Most of them are unaware of how to handle affection from those who they have mistreated. In grade school, one of the ways it has been shown is through gifts. Maybe it is through a kind word. Sometimes it is witnessed by helping them with a task. It is not that different in adulthood. It may not be as formal or as blatantly obvious, but it is there.

As adults, we can still show it through gifts. When that frustrating neighbor runs out of gas mowing the lawn, take the initiative to offer some of yours. When the rude coworker forgets a pen, make sure you have an extra in your pocket. And every Christmas, get the mean relative a good gift.

When you see the neighbor come out of his home, offer him a greeting. Wave to him if you see him in town. Tell that coworker they did a good job. Remind that relative that they are not just family in name only.

And if you see that neighbor lifting furniture, offer a helping hand. If that coworker is swamped, offer to take a little off their plate, and if you see that family member fall on hard times, do not be afraid to reach out and give a little assistance.

Treating others with kindness is a rule that all of us know. I do not even have to say what the golden rule is. Still, all of us know it by heart. The "doing unto others" counts for bullies as well. They are just as human as you. And think about it from that perspective. Have you readily shown anger to those who have given you kindness? Is it not difficult to hate those who have given you love? Kindness, grace, and blessings are things we should give to each other. The result is reflective. That which we give to others is normally returned.

LORD, I KNOW IT IS EASY FOR ME TO HOLD ON TO BITTERNESS AGAINST THOSE WHO HAVE WRONGED ME. I KNOW THERE ARE TIMES WHEN I FIND IT SO EASY TO HATE THOSE WHO HAVE SHOWN HATE TO ME. REMIND ME TO LOVE MY ENEMIES, LORD. REMIND ME THAT LOVE IS NOT SOMETHING THAT IS KEPT SECRET, BUT IS GIVEN TO OTHERS. AMEN.

30

LAZINESS IS NOT STILLNESS

How long will you stay in bed, you slacker?
When will you get up from your sleep?

PROVERBS 6:9

The first step to repentance is confession. We all do it. Every single one of us, whether it is often or rare, falls to the temptation of laziness. Some would argue that sloth is probably the most common of the seven deadly sins. And in this day and age, it is one of the most culturally acceptable sins that we regularly commit. Rest is necessary. Peace has a purpose, but when stillness morphs into laziness, we find ourselves in very unhealthy territory.

For some, it may be an electronic distraction. Our bodies may be still, and the only part of us that may be moving is the swiping of fingertips, but just because our heart rate might be low and our breathing may be steady does not mean that we are still. As our eyes dart back from up, down, left, and right to read and view various posts, our minds do not find a place of stillness. That video game is all well and good for an hour or so, but many teenagers and some adults will waste hours of their lives twiddling their thumbs. Or maybe you have let your television know that you are, indeed, still there and can watch "just one more" episode.

Maybe your distraction is centered on rest itself. We all know someone who brags about the ability to sleep for hours on end. They might say things like "I'm a professional napper," or "Sometimes I'll sleep when I'm not even that tired." Even though sleep is incredibly important, using it as a regular escape is not a way to live, and it is not the practice of being still.

And in that last statement, we find the point of today's message. Stillness is a practice. Being still, as strange as it may sound, requires a certain level of discipline. We are not still when we use rest as a form of escapism. We are not at peace when we scroll through social media, when we watch episode after episode, or when our virtual selves are trying to save the world.

In all honesty, taking a nap after a busy day is not a bad thing. Catching up with what our friends and family are doing does not make us an immoral person and watching one's favorite show or playing a video game as a way to unwind is not sinful, but we should not substitute these with stillness. Stillness comes from prayer, from studying one's Bible, and from meditating on our prayer time or our Bible study. It is acceptable to go after things that may quiet the body or relax the mind, but spending time with God is the only thing that stills the soul.

LORD, I ADMIT I HAVE BEEN LAZY. I KNOW THERE HAVE BEEN TIMES WHEN I HAVE ALLOWED DISTRACTION AND ESCAPISM TO REPLACE TRUE STILLNESS. ALLOW ME TO FIND PEACE WITH YOU. REMIND ME TO SEEK YOU SO I MAY KNOW TRUE STILLNESS AND AVOID LAZINESS. AMEN.

31

THE QUIET IN THE FIGHT

**For God has not given us a spirit of fear, but
one of power, love, and sound judgment.**

2 TIMOTHY 1:7

Fighting does not seem very Christian. It is a bit strange to find it in a book about stillness, and yet, martial artists have learned the importance of it all over the world. No matter the form, whether it be Tae Kwon Do, Jiu-Jitsu, Tai Chi, Kung Fu, or Judo, it is imperative for martial artists to learn stillness. They do so through two forms of training: physical and mental.

On the physical side, a martial artist's body endures grueling training. It is not acceptable for them to be adept only at cardiovascular fitness; they need to be incredibly strong as well. Before any technique is shared, the body molds to handle the stress of training. Even though sweat and blood are sacrificed during this preparation process, many fighters will claim that this is the easiest part of the learning process.

Once the student has prepared their body, he or she undergoes technique and sparring. Through technical training, the fighter learns methods and becomes familiar with the proper way to handle certain situations. Depending on how an opponent moves, an avid martial artist will have studied and performed the appropriate technique countless times. Through sparring, students become familiar with the unpredictable nature of an opponent. A blend of both technical study, as well as unpredictable application, will create a strong fighter.

This training is tested in competition. And in the fight, a competitor learns the real prize of proper training. When in the moment of confrontation, a person who has not taken the time to prepare their body and mind will notice that they are ill-equipped to take on their opponent. Their heart rate rises. Their senses heighten, and even though they may be a better athlete, their nervousness will get the better of them every time.

What a skilled martial artist learns is that it is not about the technique or the athleticism that wins the fight. Even though those are needed elements, the one with the calm demeanor will be the one who finds victory.

In life, we find a striking similarity. Think about it. How much energy do you waste when you panic? How often does defeat come when you feel unprepared for the task at hand? Whether we have not taken the time to prepare or have not trained our minds to take on obstacles confidently, we must remember who we are. We are children of God. We were not given a spirit of fear. Instead, we were made to be powerful, to love ferociously, and to think soundly.

HEAVENLY FATHER, I HAVE COWERED IN FEAR AT THE THINGS THAT ARE IN FRONT OF ME. I HAVE ALLOWED FEAR TO CREEP IN AND CAUSE ME TO LOSE MY COOL IN SITUATIONS THAT NEEDED IT. REMIND ME TO PUT MY FAITH IN YOU. REMIND ME THAT YOU HAVE MADE MY SPIRIT POWERFUL, FILLED WITH LOVE, AND JUDGES SOUNDLY. AMEN.

32

A GOOD WOMAN

**A man who finds a wife finds a good thing
and obtains favor from the LORD.**

PROVERBS 18:22

Kenneth was wild. As a child, teachers knew him as the playful troublemaker. As a teenager, he was the boy most fathers did not want dating their daughters. And as a young man, he wandered from place to place, traveling for work and enjoying the freedom of escaping a small town. He came home on the holidays and for birthdays, but he spent most of his time exploring different parts of the world. There was, however, one girl who held his infatuation: the pastor's daughter.

When Kenneth was home for an extended stay, he bumped into this young woman at the grocery store. When he graduated high school and left for college, she was a sophomore who was the epitome of what he assumed was a childish crush. When he returned, she was now one of the leading teachers in the county, and still just as striking as she always was. From that encounter, the two would start to date. Kenneth would try to impress her with this lavish lifestyle: fancy dinners, nice cars, he even tried to take her on a few work trips, but she insisted that she does not go on overnight trips with men who are not her husband.

After three months of dating, Kenneth started noticing that he was leaving less and less and was staying longer and longer. He was able to do his job from anywhere. So, why would he want to do it in the small, unknown town where he was raised? And yet, he found himself longing to be near the pastor's daughter. Finally, after a few more months of dating, he sat down with the pastor and asked for his blessing to pursue his daughter for marriage.

He found the man sitting on the back patio with an empty chair next to him. He stood when he arrived and greeted Kenneth. He then guided him to his seat and started a fire as the sun began to set. Kenneth abruptly and nervously started explaining his intentions. The pastor lovingly shushed him and asked him to wait until the fire was at its full flame. Kenneth tried again, but the pastor silenced him once more—saying that the fire was not high enough yet. Kenneth sensed a lesson coming, so he sat back and waited for his potential father-in-law to speak.

"You've always been a fire, Kenneth . . . ever-changing, never the same, and providing tremendous warmth. I've known you've liked my daughter for quite some time. But you are a flame, my daughter needs a rock. She needs a man that is going to stand by her. She needs a man that is going to lead her. As you are now, you give her entertainment and affection, but love is steady and never dies like this flame eventually will." Kenneth was dejected. He assumed that this conversation was leading to a refusal.

"I was a fire," the pastor said. "God gave me a good woman to remind me that I needed to be a rock. Because of the goodness of my wife, I have learned to be a rock for many. Treat my daughter well, and she will teach you how to be a rock for her and others."

HEAVENLY FATHER, THERE ARE TIMES WHEN I WANDER WILDLY. STEADY ME. TEACH ME TO LOVE OTHERS WELL AND TO SHOW THE SAME STEADY STILLNESS FOR THEM. AMEN.

THE SUNROOM

*So they went away in the boat by
themselves to a remote place.*

MARK 6:32

Elizabeth is a woman of simple tastes. When she and her husband had finally saved enough money to do some home renovations, she was not looking to be glamorous. She cared about the kitchen, of course, and she wanted a walk-in closet, and if there was enough money, she wanted to update the bathroom to get rid of the tile that had been there since the 1970s. For most couples, this list was typical. There was nothing out of the ordinary.

When they hired a contractor, she and her husband made a "Have to Have" list and an "If There's Extra" list. On the "Have to Have" list, Elizabeth and her husband listed an updated kitchen, a walk-in closet, and an updated bathroom. Both of them planned out the budget for those things. But on the "If There's Extra" list, they listed a study and a sunroom. The study would serve as an office for her husband. The sunroom would serve as a place to read and watch sunsets for her. They both expected that there should be enough for both of them, but they did not want to get their hopes up too high.

As with any home project, however, something went wrong. Pipes needed replacing. Mold formed behind the drywall, and the countertops they wanted were more expensive because fewer places were selling them nearby. Suddenly, this planned expenditure started becoming more and more chaotic.

The two then started looking at the list. They were correct in one regard. There was going to be enough money for the "Have to Have" list, but it seemed that there was only going to be enough in the budget to have either the study or the sunroom.

Elizabeth loved her husband. He worked hard for the family, and because of his work, she was able to stay home with the kids. His job now had him working from home. In her mind, the study was the obvious choice. The last weeks of renovation passed, and when work was supposed to start on the study, Elizabeth was shocked to find men building a sunroom where her back patio used to be. She turned to find her husband smiling at her as he said, "Offices are so stuffy. Besides, we both need a place to be still when the day ends."

So often, we find places to work. How often do we find places to rest? Work is good, but instead of focusing on a place to work hard, find a place to rest well.

LORD, I KNOW THERE ARE TIMES WHEN I PUT SO MUCH EMPHASIS ON FINDING A PLACE TO WORK. I KNOW IT IS EQUALLY IMPORTANT FOR ME TO FIND A PLACE TO REST. I FORGET THAT FROM TIME TO TIME. PLEASE REMIND ME TO HAVE A SAFE PLACE TO RECHARGE, RELAX, AND BE STILL. AMEN.

SHOE FOAM

Will you not revive us again so that your people may rejoice in you?

PSALM 85:6

If you were to go to any shoe store, any runner would tell you that it is wise to purchase two pairs of shoes. It may seem like a cheap trick to get someone to buy more apparel, but it turns out there may be a little bit of truth in their guidance. It is actually smart to buy an extra pair of running shoes.

Essentially, when we run, the weight of our bodies comes down on our bodies. I am sure that at this point you are wondering when the wisdom is going to come. Well, with every step, the full weight of our bodies slams through our feet onto the shoe. And if we remember the laws of physics we learned in high school, every action has an equal and opposite reaction. So, as two hundred pounds of pressure comes from our bodies to the top of the shoe, the concrete gives back the same force to the bottom of the shoe. The foam in the shoe compresses and becomes thinner every time we run. Now, if we run every other day, the foam will come a little bit closer to its original form, but if we are running every day, the foam becomes thinner and thinner.

What does this all mean? It means that even though running shoes are for, well, running, they lose their ability to cushion our feet quickly if we do not give them time to revive a bit. Many runners will even buy shoes specifically for their race day simply because they want the foam in the shoe to be as fresh as possible. Once a shoe has lost its ability to take on some of the steady impacts of concrete, it can be dangerous to run long distances.

Even though we are discussing shoes, maybe you are finding that you have a little bit in common with running shoes. Did you ever look at your shoes and feel a sense of understanding? Are you run down? Are your laces loose because they have been pulled too tight far too many times? Is your foam running a little thin?

In life, there are so many times that we need to be still for a bit. We run ourselves ragged. Whether it be taking care of the kids or performing a task for work, if we do not take time to recharge our batteries, we will find out that the foam of the body, mind, and soul is running a little too thin to continue using.

HEAVENLY FATHER, I AM TIRED. I DO NOT KNOW A BETTER WAY TO SAY IT. I HAVE BEEN RUNNING AND RUNNING ON ENERGY THAT I JUST DO NOT HAVE. GIVE ME REST, LORD. ALLOW ME TO RECHARGE AND REVIVE MY SPIRITS SO I MAY GLORIFY YOU. AMEN.

35

THE TRAIN RIDE HOME

"Come to me, all of you who are weary and burdened, and I will give you rest."

MATTHEW 11:28

Sarah lives in New Jersey but works in New York. This is not uncharacteristic. Thousands of Americans look at New Jersey as having some of the best bedroom communities for those who work in the city. When Sarah was in her early twenties, all she wanted to do was work and live in the Big Apple. She was only able to fulfill half of that dream. Even though Sarah loves working in New York City, finding an affordable apartment is unlikely. She was only able to do this for a year and had to have four roommates to do it, and according to her, it is not as glamorous as television makes it out to be.

Even though it is not Manhattan, Sarah has learned to love the little three-bedroom house she calls home, and because she is an editor, Sarah only has to come into the office once or twice a week. If it is a big week at work, she will sometimes stay overnight with a few friends, but her favorite part of her life split between the big city and suburbia is the commute. She loves the train ride to and from work. She gets up early, pours coffee into her thermos, and drives to the train station to leave her car and ride into the city.

While on the train to work, she listens to music and watches the sunrise as she sips her coffee. She takes in the coming morning and prepares herself for a day of hard work. While on the train home, she allows her eyes to shut for a few moments and takes in a few deep breaths to prepare her body and mind for rest once she arrives home. Even though there are two styles of mental preparation, they both center around similar strategies: meditation and stillness.

The hour-long train ride gives Sarah time on the way to work to quietly remove all of the distractions of the day before and focus on the job ahead. On the other hand, the ride back home gives her an hour to let go of the stress built from the day. She stills her mind and meditates on what she has learned. Because of a train, she is afforded the ability to trust that she will get where she needs to go. She does not have to worry about driving or missing her stop. She sits, rests, and quiets the soul to prepare for a long day and decompresses after the day has finally ended. We do not always have the luxury of a train car to do the driving for us. But finding an hour in each day to rest the busy mind before and after a long day at work is imperative.

LORD, I KNOW THERE ARE SO MANY TIMES THAT I LET THE BUSYNESS OF THE DAY KEEP ME FROM PREPARING FOR IT AND DECOMPRESSING FROM IT. GIVE ME TIME TO FIND REST. REMIND ME TO MAKE TIME FOR STILLNESS IN YOUR PRESENCE. AMEN.

THE REST OF AN EXTROVERT

Two are better than one because they have a
good reward for their efforts. For if either falls,
his companion can lift him up; but pity the one
who falls without another to lift him up.

ECCLESIASTES 4:9–10

It is normal to find a married couple that complements the other. For instance, you might have one who is more of a spender and one who is more naturally a saver. You might have one who values the importance of time with family, and the other may be one who places more stock in their independence. There, however, is not a more obvious dichotomy between the extrovert and the introvert. In each couple, there is one that thrives in large crowds and one that blossoms when they are left alone. There is not a clearer picture of this than in the marriage between Anna and Kavin. Anna is very much the extrovert, and even though Kavin is friendly and enjoys gathering with friends, he is the first to tell you that he loves his alone time. We will talk more about him tomorrow.

Anna, though, loves being around her friends. If there is an opportunity to get together with her "girls," she does everything in her power to make it happen. Anna loves hosting. She enjoys parties, and above all, there is something special about spending time with those who are precious to her. Many, including her husband, are often baffled how she keeps going and going and spending time with more and more people.

When asked about it, her response is simple. "Some people recharge with a good book. Some will dive into a show, and some will just go and take a nap. I love all of those things, and they give me rest, but there is something special about spending time with loved ones. In the moments when I am with my husband, my family, my friends, and my church, I do more than rest. I recharge."

We often forget the value of a friend when it comes down to finding rest. Sometimes stillness is not about the actual state of being still. Sometimes it is more about finding a safe place. For our introverted friends, a safe place can feel a little more secluded. But for our extroverts, stillness is found in the presence of safe people. A good friend who they can count on can bring a level of peace that overflows the soul and pours out into a state where they feel they can be still and know that they are safe in the presence of a loved one.

HEAVENLY FATHER, THANK YOU FOR FRIENDS AND FAMILY. THERE ARE SO MANY MOMENTS WHEN I FEEL I DO NOT PRAY FOR THEM THE WAY THAT I SHOULD. THANK YOU FOR PLACING THEM IN MY LIFE. THANK YOU FOR ALLOWING THEM TO BE A SOURCE OF PEACE AND SAFETY. REMIND ME THAT EVEN THOUGH THEY ARE A PLACE OF REFUGE, YOU ARE THE TRUE REFUGE THAT I NEED AND SHOULD SEEK. AMEN.

37

THE REST OF AN INTROVERT

*"But when you pray, go into your private room, shut
your door, and pray to your Father who is in secret.
And your Father who sees in secret will reward you."*

MATTHEW 6:6

Yesterday, we discussed Anna, the extrovert who discovered safety and stillness in the presence of loved ones. Today, we get a sneak peek into the life of Kavin. Sneak is the proper word for this. He is a man who enjoys laughter, good times with friends, a great meal with loved ones, and is always available to watch the game with the guys. But unlike his wife, his tank empties the more and more he is around people. Her tank fills in the presence of people. To recharge, Kavin finds escape in a secret place of rest.

The place itself is not so secret. It is the garage. In their new home, he made sure that it was a three-car garage so that he could place a workbench and a home gym in it. When he goes to the garage, he inadvertently communicates to his wife, "I have had enough people today . . ." Sometimes he will go in there, listen to some music, and tinker with his car. Sometimes he will sneak in a workout while the kids take their naps.

Even though the garage has become his lair when the world has spun a bit too quickly, he escapes to other places when he deals with serious matters. When he is reading up on something for work, he removes himself from the chaos of screaming children. When he is doing Bible study, he reclines in his chair in the early morning so that he will not be distracted. And when he prays, Kavin wanders to the closet from time to time to have a serious talk with the Lord.

It is interesting to watch him because he is a welcoming person. He is warm, friendly, and has a laugh that can be identified by anyone who has heard it at least once. Many do not believe that he is an introvert. But if you ask his wife, she will be the first to tell you he needs his space at the end of a long day. For him to be able to find rest, he needs to shut off the social part of his personality and take a few breaths on his own.

Many of us forget the value of getting away on our own. We do not acknowledge the benefit of seeking seclusion. The Bible is clear on the matter. We are surrounded by distraction, and yet, God tells us to seek Him in secret. The distractions of the world are like bees buzzing around one's head. It does not matter how diligent we are. When distractions are buzzing about, it is impossible to be still before the Lord.

LORD, GOD, I KNOW THERE HAVE BEEN TIMES WHERE I HAVE TRIED TO SQUEEZE YOU IN BETWEEN THE DISTRACTIONS. I HAVE SAID A PRAYER HERE. I HAVE STUDIED YOUR WORD THERE, BUT I RARELY TAKE THE TIME TO FOCUS SOLELY ON YOU. FORGIVE ME OF THAT AND REMIND ME TO SEEK YOU IN SECRET SO MY ATTENTION IS UNDIVIDED, AND I CAN FOCUS ON YOU. AMEN.

38

STREETLIGHTS

For you are all children of light and children of the day. We do not belong to the night or the darkness.
1 THESSALONIANS 5:5

Alison has a strict policy when it comes down to when the children should be home. It is a rule that many of us have heard of and some have probably followed. Alison makes many rules, but there is not one that is more important for her twelve-year-old son and thirteen-year-old son; they have to come home when the streetlights come on. For the boys, they, at first, agreed with the rule because they can stay out later during the summer, and no one wants to be out in the middle of the winter. But as they grew older, they started to find a problem with the rule.

They noticed that their friends did not have to go home right when the streetlights started to come on. They found out that many of them had curfews that allowed them to stay out until nine and ten. When this news became apparent to them, the boys began negotiating with their mother. Alison was no negotiator. Negotiations have an element of giving and taking, and Alison was not going to yield on this one. The boys wanted a curfew like the rest of their friends. Alison's only offering is they could have one when they had driver's licenses.

This news frustrated the boys, and even though their friendships were important to them, they knew that their mother was not going to budge. After a few days of being mocked by their friends for having to go home early, Alison explained why her rule is the way that it is.

She asked her sons if any of their friends had ever gotten into trouble. They said, "Of course. All kids get in trouble!" She admitted that they had a point. She then asked about the funniest times that their friends got in trouble. Her eldest told of a time when one friend got in trouble for playing flashlight tag in the park. Her youngest spoke of a time when his friend broke a window playing baseball. She asked if either instance had anything in common with the other.

The boys' faces lowered—realizing what had been pointed out. Both occurrences happened at night, and Alison's sons were not around to see it. She asked them how many times they have gotten into trouble playing with their friends. The boys could not think of any instances outside of the occasional request to get off of one's lawn. Her response, "Nighttime is the playground for trouble. Boys that are not using the night to rest, normally use it for mischief."

LORD, THANK YOU FOR THE EVENING. I KNOW I DO NOT THANK YOU ENOUGH FOR SETTING ASIDE A TIME EVERY DAY TO REST. WHEN I AM NOT RESTING, LORD, I KNOW THERE IS A CHANCE FOR ME TO GET INTO TROUBLE. ALLOW ME TO RECOGNIZE THE IMPORTANCE OF REST WHEN THE SUN GOES DOWN AND REMIND ME TO AVOID MOMENTS THAT GET ME INTO TROUBLE. AMEN.

39

CHANGING TECHNOLOGY

Jesus Christ is the same yesterday, today, and forever.

HEBREWS 13:8

Robert has been in the technology business for more than forty years. Admittedly, he has mainly been on the business side of the technology business. With the ever-changing nature of technology, it is strange to see his white hair walking around the office. Young adults are seen at every turn, creating new concepts, new technologies, and applications that make our current technology move with more efficiency. He has seen every major movement in the technology industry over the past four decades.

He was in charge of making the first mobile computer marketable. Sure, it was thirty pounds and had a screen the size of one's palm, but for the first time, you could type anywhere. When cell phones were the size of one's head, he came up with ways to make the phone appear easily portable. He helped customers understand the versatility that came with having a full keyboard that slides out of the bottom of a cell phone. And when computers evolved from megabytes to gigabytes, he was able to market the need for such space on hard drives. He has seen the movement of putting computers in pockets, unlimited access to music through phones, and social media that allows conversations with strangers from all over the world.

With every changing movement in technology, he has watched college degrees become trinkets and witnessed innovators crawl out of garages. It is no surprise that he gets a couple of raised eyebrows when he walks onto the elevator. Employees benefit from living in a time when they can wear what they want to work. Some men have hair down to their shoulders and wear flip-flops with dress pants. Some women have blue streaks in their hair and facial piercings. But as for Robert, he comes to work with khakis, a dress shirt, and a tie every day.

One day, one of the young employees wandered over to his section of the office and built up the nerve to ask, "Robert, what do you know about technology?" He smiled a bit and said, "The only thing I know about technology is that it is always changing. Five years from now, the innovation you are creating will be obsolete." The young man looked insulted, but Robert relented and said with more grace. "You have the adventure in creating something new every day. I live in the comfort of knowing that though what we sell may change frequently, the art of business rarely does."

In life, we see the world spinning, and each new season bringing new challenges and obstacles. Even though the world is ever-changing, as Christians, we live in the stillness and peace in knowing that our Savior is the same in every occurrence.

LORD JESUS, THANK YOU FOR NEVER CHANGING. THANK YOU FOR CONSTANTLY LOVING ME. IN MOMENTS WHERE I HAVE PROVEN THAT I DO NOT DESERVE IT, YOU HAVE STILL SHOWN YOUR LOVE AND GRACE TO ME. REMIND ME OF THE NEVER-CHANGING NATURE OF YOUR LOVE, AND ALLOW ME TO SHARE THAT LOVE WITH OTHERS. AMEN.

GRACE UPON GRACE

Indeed, we have all received grace
upon grace from his fullness.

JOHN 1:16

One of the most challenging concepts to discuss with the unchurched is the principle of grace. It is something that many of us know that we have, but we forget just how bountiful this gift is. To be given grace is something that we all understand. How many of us have forgiven someone easily? When there is love for the person, it is a little easier for us to show grace. The reason for this is because we know that people we love would not want to harm us intentionally. On the other side of that kind of grace, how many of us have found it difficult to forgive someone? When someone difficult to love commits a wrong against us, we somehow convince ourselves that this person did so with some form of intentionality. Here's the worst part to hear: in the eyes of God, we are more like the latter than the former.

Because of this, many Christians wrestle with whether or not they have grace because they do not deserve it. The truth is that they are half correct and half wrong. God's grace is not given to us because we deserve it. Based on our works, it would be impossible for us to earn any notion of forgiveness. Because of our human nature, we so desperately wish that our actions were somehow enough to get us at least a little bit of the way there. This kind of belief is faulty. God gives His love freely. There is nothing we can do to earn it.

This revelation causes two reactions in the hearts of almost every Christian: peace and anxiety. The anxious part of us still wishes that we could make God love us because we assume we are lovable, but the peaceful side of us gives us freedom in knowing that God loves us because He is love. His grace is given on top of more grace.

So what does this have to do with stillness? What does this have to do with finding rest? Well, if you have made it this far in the book, I can only assume that you are likely a Christian. Maybe, like so many others, you are wondering how God could ever love you. This thought may have kept you up at night. You may have lost sleep wondering if you deserve God's love. Well, I am here to tell you that you do not. There is nothing you could ever do to ever earn God's love. And yet, He loves you anyway. He sent His Son to die for you, and even now, with every bad thing you have done since meeting Him, He loves you still.

LORD, I KNOW I DO NOT DESERVE YOUR LOVE, AND YOU STILL CHOOSE TO LOVE ME. THANK YOU FOR THAT LOVE. AS I FIND REST, ALLOW ME TO PLACE IT IN THE KNOWLEDGE OF KNOWING HOW MUCH YOU LOVE ME. AMEN.

STUDYING IN
THE LIBRARY

Very early in the morning, while it was still dark, he got up, went out, and made his way to a deserted place; and there he was praying.

Chances are, you have probably been in a library at least once in your life. Whether you studied in one as a student in high school or visited one as an adult, you have most likely observed the towering shelves filled with countless books written on subjects you could probably never begin to fathom. What is most notable about these temples of knowledge is not necessarily the books inside. After all, the New York library has a collection few libraries can rival. What every library has in common, however, is the atmosphere of the buildings themselves. They are not places for outbursts or loud conversations, nor are they places for heated discussions or raised voices. Instead, libraries are collectively known for their stillness.

They are the kind of places that create reading nooks where one can dive into a different world of fantasy and adventure. They are the kind of buildings with thick wooden tables that allow students to grab multiple textbooks for in-depth study. It is not a playground for the body but is a sanctuary for the mind. This is not possible if they are filled with loud and unpredictable environments.

Their primary benefit is not the collection of tomes collected over the decades, nor is it their sturdy furniture upon which a student can lay out a vast array of books for study. Their greatest benefit is not even found in their complete collections of encyclopedias or dictionaries, or the ever-aging card catalog. No, a library's greatest benefit is the peaceful and quiet environment it offers to students of all types. It is non-discriminatory to those in search of knowledge. Its gift to any who enter through its door is a promise that a reader's time in the building will not be disturbed by uninvited noise.

In life, many of us forget the benefit of escaping to a quiet place. We misplace the importance of finding not only a time of silence but also a place to be silent. We know the importance of doing so when it comes down to study. After all, there is little worth in studying the loud moments, but we often ignore how good our prayer time can be if it is one that is filled with silence.

Christ gave us this example. He understood that in order to have a proper conversation with His Father, He had to be willing to be in a quiet place to listen to what God would have Him hear. We cannot forget that. So, just as it is important for you to study in the quiet, do not forget its importance in the moments of your prayers.

HEAVENLY FATHER, I KNOW I HAVE NOT GIVEN YOU THE PROPER ATMOSPHERE WHEN I HAVE COME TO YOU IN PRAYER. I HAVE TRIED TO FIT YOU INTO THE CHAOS INSTEAD OF REMOVING MYSELF FROM IT TO BE WITH YOU. REMIND ME TO PUT YOU FIRST AND FIND TIME TO BE WITH YOU. AMEN.

42

BEING DOUBLE-MINDED

Draw near to God, and he will draw near
to you. Cleanse your hands, sinners, and
purify your hearts, you double-minded.

JAMES 4:8

To be double-minded in its simplest form is to be inconsistent, vacillating, or to act one way in one place and a different way in another. The reality is that many of us have observed these individuals in their most extreme forms. They may be the person who can pray a poem to God but will not walk the path God has given them the moment they leave the church building. They may be the person who knows the Bible frontward and backward but do not take the time to live by any word that they likely have memorized. Sadly, even in the most extreme cases of the double-minded nature of those frustrating few, we forget to stop, take a breath, and look in the mirror to find one of the most double-minded individuals we know: ourselves.

It is rarely a chore for us to identify the flaws in others, but we rarely take the time to acknowledge the issues that we face on our own. We assume that because these individuals are so far from perfection that we must, somehow, be closer. This is not the case. As difficult as it is for some of us to realize, we are often just as double-minded as those we point to as prime suspects. We are right there with them in the line-up of criminals who have acted against a loving Father.

To be clear, this is not to bring swift condemnation to the hearts of those who are reading this. Instead, this writing is here to readjust our focus from our ivory towers of moral superiority and recognize that we reside in the slums with everyone else. It exists to readjust us in the quiet. You are likely reading this at bedtime or in the early morning when the chaos of the day has either finished for the day or not started yet. It is because of this quiet that I encourage you to reflect.

Think about your life for a moment. Are there areas in your life where you have been double-minded? Of course, you may not be as conspicuous as the family that arrives at church late. You might not be the person that has a harsh word for your loved ones, but maybe you are the one who has wished ill of those that drive poorly. Perhaps you have reveled in the fantasy of proving someone wrong. Whatever the case may be, use this moment of stillness to reflect on the moments you have been double-minded and give them to God for forgiveness and correction.

LORD, I ADMIT THERE ARE MORE MOMENTS THAN I WOULD CARE TO COUNT WHEN I HAVE ACTED SELFISHLY. I HAVE BEEN DOUBLE-MINDED EVEN IN MY VIEW OF OTHERS. PLEASE, ALLOW ME TO SEEK YOU AND LIVE A LIFE THAT IS SINGULARLY FOCUSED ON YOU INSTEAD OF LIVING ONE SEPARATELY. AMEN.

43

THE PEACE OF A
HELPING HAND

"If you see your brother's donkey or ox fallen down
on the road, do not ignore it; help him lift it up."

DEUTERONOMY 22:4

Jasper is nearly seven feet tall, a little over two hundred and seventy pounds, and plays on the practice squad for one of the teams in the national football league. To say that he is an imposing figure is an understatement. He is an enormous man with an even larger presence. Upon first meeting him, many fight lumps in their throats when approaching the giant man. But for those who know him even a little, they are quick to tell you he is one of the kindest souls you could ever come to know.

Every morning, he wakes up and goes for a run before working out in his makeshift gym in his garage. As a professional athlete, he can afford the big house and the fancy car in the rich neighborhood, but as a way to save money, he lives in a moderately upper-middle-class neighborhood in a nice house but nothing too showy. He lives comfortably but as a guy who grew up in a small town in a poor community, he was not chomping at the bit to be surrounded by the ultra-wealthy.

Now and again, he will see a new family moving into the neighborhood. He will offer a wave, a smile, and any help they may need with heavy furniture. Most people not, wanting to bother him, will normally wave back and assure him that they have everything under control, but occasionally, he'll get the chance to use his strength for something other than running into people.

His newest neighbors are an elderly couple who moved into their dream home upon retirement. Both of them in their early sixties pulled up in the huge moving van, and Jasper watched in amazement as the two started unloading everything they could together. Other neighbors eventually showed up and started helping the couple, and Jasper would offer to as well. The husband immediately recognized the name and stature of Jasper and remarked that he played for his favorite team in the league. Jasper offered his giant hand for a handshake and asked how he could help.

The couple scratched their heads and remarked that the only thing they could not figure out how to move was their wardrobe. It was sturdy and did not have to be handled delicately, but it was definitely bulky. Jasper offered a grin and walked over to the piece and hoisted it onto his back and walked into the home. The couple cheered his efforts and admitted that even though they were grateful for all the help they had been given, they were terrified because it took four college students to be able to get it onto the truck in the first place. They had no idea how they would get it off.

There is a certain peace that comes from receiving help in times of need. There are going to be moments when assistance is necessary, and we cannot do it on our own. When those moments come, and they will, praise God for the peace that comes from a helping hand and offer it to those who are in need as well.

LORD, THANK YOU FOR PROVIDING ME WITH THOSE WHO OFFER A HELPING HAND. REMIND ME TO OFFER THE SAME TO THOSE WHEN THEY ARE IN NEED AS WELL. AMEN.

STILLNESS OF A HYMN

Sing to him, sing praise to him;
tell about all his wondrous works!

PSALM 105:2

There is a church in the Nashville area that has moved with the times of the music city. This is not out of the ordinary. Many churches modernize to attract younger crowds to fill the seats of the sanctuary. Some even go as far as ripping up wine-colored carpets and paint walls to give the building a fresh new look that will stand out to visitors as they enter the building. A church needs to communicate that it is just as focused on spreading the gospel in the present as it was in the past. Sometimes, that requires updates.

There, however, has not been a more contentious issue in this movement than that of the changing of the style of musical worship. Organs are replaced with electric keyboards. A choir loft is now a place for the percussion team. Instead of a worship leader waving his hand to the congregation to guide them musically, we find who that strums a guitar and sings songs of familiarity. And instead of cracking open the hymnal and singing from a book, words are projected onto a screen for all to see as they worship God. To say that the change has not been a drastic one of the past couple of decades would be an ignorant statement.

Many older members of the congregations will feel disenfranchised and forgotten with the move toward the modern. They will assume that their preferred style of worship is now irrelevant in the face of the new musical movement. They do not see the use of shouting repetitive messages to the heavens, and because of their lack of interest in the new style of music, they assume they are unwanted in the congregation.

Even in all of this frustration, however, there is an agreement upon the notion of a well-done hymn. New musical styles cannot keep up with the words of old. Hymns were written with the knowledge that most churches would be lucky to have a piano in the building, let alone a full band. Because of this, the value of the words sung became paramount in the face of the music played. In the times of elders' youth, the words spoke louder than the instrument.

Because of this, the pastor of this church makes sure that every service has at least one hymn. Whenever he does this, the band stops playing except for the keyboard, and the introduction of a familiar hymn fills the room. It gives the younger crowd an appreciation for the ways of the old. But even more so, it quiets the room, and instead of instrumental music filling the sanctuary, one hears voices shouting deep theological truths in the worship of the Almighty.

ALMIGHTY GOD, I KNOW YOU ARE GREAT. I KNOW THERE ARE MOMENTS WHERE I HAVE ALLOWED THE DISTRACTION OF INSTRUMENTS TO KEEP ME FROM ACKNOWLEDGING THE WORDS I AM SINGING TO YOU. ALLOW ME TO APPRECIATE THE MUSIC BEING PLAYED, BUT STILL MY HEART AND PREPARE MY VOICE TO SING TRUTHS IN WORSHIP TO YOU. AMEN.

HEALTHY BODIES

Therefore, brothers and sisters, in view of
the mercies of God, I urge you to present
your bodies as a living sacrifice, holy and
pleasing to God; this is your true worship.

ROMANS 12:1

Many of us feel almost a hatred toward the notion of a healthy body. It can mean eating foods that we do not wish to eat or participating in an exercise that we do not want to do. Whether we admit it or not, the benefit of health does not always outweigh our desire to do unhealthy things. Regrettably, we enjoy eating greasy foods and lounging. We find a bit of pleasure in lying on the couch when we are not even that tired, or we love the possibility of eating a large meal. Indulgent behavior, however, is rarely ever something that gives long-lasting peace.

What do I mean by this? Well, think about any time you have been to a doctor. It does not matter whether it is a physician or a dentist. We are well-aware of the panic that sets in during the weeks leading up to an appointment. We start thinking about the naps we chose instead of the run we could have taken. We remember all of the foods that we ate that weaken our bodies and rot our teeth. And in that recall, we start wishing we were able to present healthy bodies to the ones who check them to make sure everything is operating the way it should.

We are rarely shocked when a diagnosis comes back negative. Having a cheeseburger every other day has never been known to *lower* one's cholesterol, and I have never heard of a professional athlete who refuses to exercise. Health is one of the few gifts of this world that the vast majority of us have some form of control over. We do not have to be unhealthy, and yet, so many of us are. Many of us live in frustration knowing that whenever we have to *present* our bodies to the ones who matter, we do not feel peace at the moment.

This is not a message to tell you to go buy whitening kits for your teeth or to go and join a gym and take on the fitness regimen of a bodybuilder, but it is to acknowledge the fact that people who take care of their bodies rarely have to deal with the frustration of being unhealthy. They often live in peace knowing that they have taken care of their bodies and can present them before doctors and dentists and know that their diagnosis will likely not be a negative one. So, take care of yourself. Your body is a gift from God, treat it like one, and recognize the peace that comes from living a life that is healthy both in spirit and body.

LORD, I KNOW THERE ARE TIMES THAT I HAVE NOT TAKEN CARE OF MYSELF IN THE WAY THAT I SHOULD. REMIND ME TO TAKE CARE OF MY BODY AND TREAT IT AS A GIFT FROM YOU. AMEN.

THE NEED FOR LAMBY

Those who cherish worthless idols abandon their faithful love.

JONAH 2:8

Spencer is an independent child. She can play by herself; she uses her imagination and doesn't need entertainment, and she enjoys a quiet home. She is the perfect child. Other parents ask Spencer's mom and dad about their secret parenting techniques. Spencer is four years old, but do not let her independent demeanor fool you. She is still very much a child. Every night when bedtime encroaches, Spencer asks for Lamby. Lamby, as you might guess, is a stuffed lamb that Spencer requests every night when she starts getting ready for bed.

Whenever her father gives her Lamby, he hoists her up and takes her to bed. He then reads her a chapter of a book they are going through together. By the end of the reading, if she is not already asleep, she is prepared to be left alone to fall asleep on her own. Just like every other stuffed animal, however, Lamby got dirty and was in dire need of a bath of his own. Because of this, Spencer's mother took Lamby and placed him in the washing machine, and said that she would have to spend the night without her stuffed toy for one evening.

This, of course, was not going to happen. Spencer refused to go to bed unless she had her Lamby. In the briefest moment, Spencer morphed from a mature, independent child, to a weeping toddler in dire need of the toy that allowed her to sleep. The washing machine had already started. There was no way that Lamby was going to be available to Spencer. As a compromise, Spencer's father offered to read two chapters of their book and would stay with her until she fell asleep. With tear-filled eyes, she nodded. Her father, once again, lifted her off the ground and carried her to her room as she rested her head on his shoulder.

When they arrived, he tucked her into bed, kissed her forehead, and began reading her story. At this moment, Spencer had a bit of a realization. After her father started reading and acting out parts in the book with silly voices, she forgot about Lamby. It was only for a moment, and she was too young to understand what was happening. But somehow, she knew that the peace of bedtime was not about having Lamby with her, but instead about spending time with her father before she fell asleep.

It sounds familiar, does it not? When we get ready for bed, we have so many rituals that bring us a bit of peace before falling to sleep, but there is nothing quite like spending time with the Father before we close our eyes and rest. Take time this evening to pray to Him, read His Word, and meditate on His love. You might be surprised at the sleep that comes from it.

LORD, I KNOW YOU ARE GOOD. FORGIVE ME FOR THE TIMES WHEN I HAVE PUT OTHER THINGS WHERE YOU SHOULD BE. REMIND ME OF YOUR GOODNESS AND KEEP MY FOCUS ON YOU. AMEN.

47

"DO YOU HEAR THAT?"

To seek to lead a quiet life, to mind your
own business, and to work with your
own hands, as we commanded you.

1 THESSALONIANS 4:11

Barry is a project manager for a local construction company. His office is in a double-wide mobile home that plants itself in front of whatever work site he finds himself. He handles payroll for the other workers, makes sure that deadlines are met, and communicates with other contractors to ensure everything remains on schedule. Barry loves his job. The money is good. He has a great camaraderie with his team, and he enjoys seeing physical reminders of the work that he has accomplished. There is one thing, however, that he hates: the noise. And with him working on a construction site, he cannot exactly escape it.

His company has tried. They have supplied him with noise-canceling headphones, insulated walls that dampen sound, and even offered him flexible scheduling that grants him the ability to work during quieter hours. Nothing has yet overcome the unending noise of a worksite. Barry, however, has come to notice the joy in getting to work a few hours earlier than the rest of his team. During this time, he and another worker will come into the office before the sun rises and take care of any paperwork that needs to be filed before the day begins. They will normally get in two or three hours of work before the rest of the team arrives.

Every morning, Barry gets out of his car, walks into his office, starts a pot of coffee, and turns on his computer. When his associate gets to the office, the two of them will get to work while the coffee brews and the bubbling and pouring of coffee is the only sound they can hear. This early-morning ritual has become a rhythm for the two of them. So much so that every morning, Barry asks his coworker the same thing. "Do you hear that?" He will ask. "Hear what?" his partner will respond. "Exactly . . ."

There can be an unspoken celebration in the quiet, a joy that does not need loud acknowledgment. We can look at the gift of stillness and enjoy that many times that the gift of stillness is often the ability to move forward without distraction. Whenever a busy day is on the horizon, do not look at it with contempt and try to figure out how to work through it. Instead, take advantage of the quiet you have now and work on what you can before the busyness comes.

LORD, I KNOW THAT RIGHT NOW I AM IN A BUSY SEASON. PLEASE ALLOW ME TO FIND THE QUIET, AND WORK IN THOSE MOMENTS WITHOUT DISTRACTION. REMIND ME TO VIEW THE QUIET MOMENTS AS GIFTS THAT YOU HAVE PROVIDED, AND REMIND ME TO GIVE THAT TIME TO THE WORK YOU WOULD HAVE ME DO. AMEN.

48

KNITTING CLUB

"For where two or three are gathered together
in my name, I am there among them."

MATTHEW 18:20

Churches have a nasty habit of counting every gathering as a fellowship. Just because people gather does not mean that they are taking part in the community. They may be enjoying each other's company and may even all be Christians, but many pastors have started to argue every gathering may not be a fellowship. It is because of this that the pastor was a bit reluctant to allow a group of women to start a knitting club. When one of the older women of the church approached the pastor about the notion of the club, he was not too keen on the idea of recognizing it as one of the community groups of the church.

The woman's reasoning for the group allowed the pastor enough wiggle room to allow it to exist as one of the groups. It also helped that her husband was chairman of the deacons. The concept was a simple one. Her idea would be to encourage women in the church to learn a skill while doing a Bible study and prayer time together on Wednesday afternoons. This was not an issue for the pastor. After all, he was in the church building all day on Wednesdays. It made sense for a group to meet before Wednesday night activities.

When it first began, the pastor paid it little attention. For the first couple of months, the ten women who attended it were above the age of fifty. But then something interesting happened. A few of the youth girls started attending. He noticed high school girls following the women with knitting supplies. A few weeks later, young mothers and college students started attending as well. Before long, women of all ages were attending the club, and now the deacon's wife was asking if they could expand their meeting space into the sanctuary. Whether the pastor liked it or not, he could not deny that whatever they were doing was cross-generational.

One afternoon, he walked by the room to peek at what was happening. What he saw astounded him. Yes, these women were teaching each other a new skill, but they saw that their creations were going to the purpose of providing hats and scarves for homeless women. The older women also taught the younger ones how to have gospel conversations with people and what parts of the Bible to lean on during their discussion.

After this, the pastor granted her request and allowed her to start meeting in the sanctuary. He never thought that something as calming and still as knitting could yield such explosive results and was excited to support it in any way that he could.

LORD, FORGIVE ME FOR THE MOMENTS WHERE I HAVE NOT BELIEVED IN THE BIG THINGS THAT YOU CAN DO IN THE QUIET MOMENTS. GIVE ME MOMENTS OF STILLNESS AND FELLOWSHIP THAT WILL ALLOW ME TO FURTHER YOUR KINGDOM. THANK YOU FOR THE GUIDANCE AND WISDOM THAT COMES FROM MY ELDERS AND REMIND ME TO SEEK YOUR WILL IN THE QUIET MOMENTS. AMEN.

49

A SAFE REMINDER

**Your word is a lamp for my feet
and a light on my path.**

PSALM 119:105

Few things are as frightening as being lost. It is a unique fear. It is not sudden like the feeling that comes from lights suddenly going off or experiencing an unexpected boom. It is a progression. Like a horror movie, the further and further someone goes into feeling out of control, the more terrifying the feeling of fear is. Whether a person finds themselves behind the wheel of a car or going out for a walk, losing one's place can be a terrifying feeling.

This is what happened to Danny as a young boy. He had been riding bikes with his friends and found himself in an unfamiliar neighborhood. It also did not help that the sun was setting and he could not see things as clearly as he once could. He started to panic. He was no longer afraid of getting in trouble. He was more fearful of simply being lost. He then remembered what his mother had always told him if he ever felt lost. She always said for him to look for the water tower. His home was within a football field's distance of the only water tower in the town.

He skimmed the horizon, still worried that he would not be able to see it in the dark, but then he saw its silhouette in the dusk sky. Upon seeing it, the fear of being lost had disappeared even though he was still in an unfamiliar area. He raced toward the water tower, and before long, other landmarks started appearing that he recognized. He saw the grocery store where his parents shopped. He saw homes with peculiar designs that let him know he was close to his neighborhood, and finally, he reached his driveway, never losing sight of the nearby water tower.

Our walk is not too different. As Christians, we wander through a world that is not familiar to us. We may be in this world, but we are certainly not of it. We recognize the safe places where we can rest, but there is no safety quite like the one felt from following the wisdom of God's Word. His Word is our familiar place. It is our safe place. Through the knowledge of God's Word, we can put our trust and follow the lit path that the Bible provides and find our way home to Him.

HEAVENLY FATHER, I RARELY THANK YOU FOR THIS, BUT THANK YOU FOR YOUR WORD. I KNOW THERE ARE TIMES WHEN I THANK YOU FOR ALL OF THE THINGS THAT YOU HAVE DONE IN MY LIFE, BUT I OFTEN FORGET TO THANK YOU FOR THE GOODNESS OF BEING ABLE TO KNOW YOU THROUGH YOUR WORD. THANK YOU FOR THE BIBLE AND CONTINUE TO ALLOW IT TO LIGHT MY PATH AND GUIDE ME FORWARD. REMIND ME THAT YOUR WORD IS A LIGHT TO MY PATH AND A LAMP TO MY FEET AND THAT IT WILL ALWAYS GUIDE ME CLOSER TO YOU. AMEN.

50

STUDYING VERSUS READING

Be diligent to present yourself to God as one approved, a worker who doesn't need to be ashamed, correctly teaching the word of truth.

2 TIMOTHY 2:15

My favorite part about the verse above is the word *correctly*. All Christians recognize the importance of reading and studying the Bible, but many only focus on one half of that equation in their daily lives. Most Christians who read the Bible daily will often admit that their daily reading of the Bible is just that, a reading. It is low-level information-gathering that sometimes sticks and sometimes does not. This does not mean that the simple reading of Scripture is a bad thing. It is only one part of the equation.

Taking in the Bible is something that should not only require introductory reading but should also include inductive study. What do I mean by this? It means looking deeply at the words on the page. This is the Word of God we are discussing. Grammar, metaphor, and other literary devices are imperative to note. If a Greek or Hebrew scholar will spend days on the importance of one word, should that not communicate the importance for us to deeply study God's Word as well?

How, then, do we accomplish this? Do we just read it at a slower pace? That is part of it, but I encourage you to find a study Bible. Make notes in it.

Write in the margins. Journal during your quiet time. Record your experiences while studying God's Word. Doing this will not only allow you to have a more profound respect for what you are reading. It will also deepen your knowledge of what you are reading.

The only way to do this, though, is to carve out time in your day to be still and dive into what you are reading. So many try to cram study time in all the chaos of our daily lives but fail to understand the benefit of finding a time to be still and study. We cannot ever hope to grow in our knowledge of God's Word if we do not take our study time seriously. Nothing ever stays in the long term memory if it is taken in during moments of chaos. So, take time to read God's Word. It is important to have a daily reminder before the day begins, but for teaching the Word of God "correctly," one must carve out the quiet and study with intentionality to yield that which God is offering.

HEAVENLY FATHER, REMIND ME TO TAKE IN DAILY MOMENTS TO READ YOUR WORD. I NEED THOSE BEFORE THE START OF ANY DAY, BUT I ALSO ASK THAT YOU INSTILL IN ME TO TAKE TIME TO DEEPLY STUDY YOUR WORD. GRANT ME MOMENTS THAT WILL GIVE ME UNINTERRUPTED TIME WITH THE BIBLE AND PUT IN ME A HEART THAT DESIRES TO KNOW MORE ABOUT YOU SO THAT I MIGHT SHARE IT WITH OTHERS IN A CORRECT WAY. GUIDE ME, LORD, AND ALLOW ME TO TEACH YOUR WORD CORRECTLY. AMEN.

51

QUIET AFTER THE STORM

He got up, rebuked the wind, and said to the sea, "Silence! Be still!" The wind ceased, and there was a great calm. Then he said to them, "Why are you afraid? Do you still have no faith?"

MARK 4:39–40

Many of us have heard the adage, "the quiet before the storm." It is a way to signal a false sense of peace before a storm rages. When the wind dies down but the clouds build, many see this as a time to take shelter and ride out whatever destruction the skies may bring. Many will hunker down in basements, hide in bathrooms, or try and find a central spot in the home. When the sirens wail and the wind causes the house to creak, many will assume that the end is near, but so many people make it out on the other side. The clouds dissipate. The sun shines, and the gusts of wind turn to peaceful breezes. And yet, many forget to carry a sense of gratitude to the God who carried us through the storm in the first place.

We always go to God in the quiet before the storm. When a project is coming up that we are not sure we are going to overcome or a responsibility is on the horizon that we are not sure we are going to be able to handle on our own, we go to God for peace to be able to carry us through it. In life, it is easy for us to go to God when there is a fear of impending doom.

When we are in the thick of it, when the storm is at our door, we go to God. We have a keen understanding of seeking out Him when the storm is coming or when we are in the middle of it, but how often do we go to God in thanksgiving for getting us on the other side of it? The reality is that there are going to be tough seasons. That is a product of the Fall, but God carries us through those seasons until we come home to Him.

When the bad times are here, seek Him as your refuge to make it through. But when the clouds part, the wind dies down, and the sun shines, thank God for calming the storm, for slowing the wind, and bringing peace into the chaos.

LORD, THANK YOU FOR PROTECTING ME WHEN THE STORM APPROACHES. THANK YOU FOR PROVIDING A REFUGE WHEN THE STORM IS HERE, AND THANK YOU FOR GIVING PEACE WHEN THE STORM IS OVER. LORD, PLEASE REMIND ME TO GO TO YOU WITH A SPIRIT OF THANKSGIVING NOT JUST WHEN I AM AFRAID OF WHAT IS TO COME OR WHAT I AM CURRENTLY DEALING WITH, BUT ALSO WHEN YOU CALM THE STORM AND PROVIDE PEACE IN MY LIFE. AMEN.

ORCHESTRA TUNING

"I will go before you and level the uneven places; I will shatter the bronze doors and cut the iron bars in two."

ISAIAH 45:2

Margaret has always loved the orchestra. As the daughter of a cellist, concert halls are just as familiar to her as stadiums are to sports fans. She enjoys all parts of the process. The music, the dressing up, the beautiful architecture, and the balcony seating are all treats to her whenever she goes. Her favorite part of attending the symphony, however, is right before the music ever starts. The lights dim. Ushers guide last-minute arrivals to their seats, and the conductor is greeted with applause as he takes his position on the platform that raises him just enough for the orchestra to see. And then, it begins.

Not the music, mind you. Margaret loves the music, but this is not what excites her. It is the tuning before the music ever starts. An oboist sets the tune, and the rest of the instruments follow suit and match the frequency the oboist has set. One after the other, each section matches the frequency. And eventually, the entire orchestra will play together, filling the concert hall with a nearly indescribable sound to those that have never heard it. And then, there is silence.

For Margaret, the tuning of the instruments and the silence that follows at a concert are her favorite parts. She reasons that before the music can ever take its first note, instruments have to be prepared and stilled. Musicians and the conductor must ensure that everything is made ready before the first swish of a baton. Once this preparation is complete, then the concert can start.

The tuning of an orchestra provides an interesting perspective to have in life. Many of us do not understand the importance of waiting on God to move in our lives. For many of us, we just want the concert to go ahead and start. Are there going to be times when life throws an unexpected curveball, and we simply have to react? Of course, but more often than not, God is working in us to prepare us for what is to come. Whether we like it or not, we need to be tuned toward Him to be able to take on the task that He has set before us.

Sometimes, our impatience keeps us from appreciating this. We want to go ahead and get on with the show. But the next time you find yourself in a season of waiting, choose to acknowledge that God may be getting ready to do something that He needs you to prepare for. So, tune your instrument. Make sure you prepare because the show may just be getting ready, and this stillness may exist with the purpose of something greater to come.

LORD, I KNOW THERE ARE SEASONS WHEN I HAVE TO WAIT. REMIND ME TO EMBRACE THE STILLNESS AND PREPARE MY SPIRIT FOR WHAT IS TO COME. ALLOW ME TO LOOK AHEAD AND TUNE MY HEART TOWARD YOUR WILL AND FOLLOW AFTER WHAT YOU WOULD HAVE FOR ME. AMEN.

53

MY SOUL TO KEEP. MY SOUL TO TAKE.

"Don't fear those who kill the body but are not able to kill the soul; rather, fear him who is able to destroy both soul and body in hell."

MATTHEW 10:28

Every night, as the sun sets and the moon rises, children all over the world prepare for bed. They take part in nightly routines that include brushing teeth, changing into pajamas, and making sure clothes are prepared for the next morning. As bedtime encroaches, however, there is a tension that occupies the minds of a few children. They know that rest is beneficial and should be pursued, but the unknown veil of unconsciousness is a notion that many young children are still seeking familiarity. Why is this apprehension there? Why do so many kids need the added comfort? Is a bedtime story necessary? Does tucking our little ones in really add that much ease? The reality is that many children need an added touch of reassurance before they enter the stage of sleep. For some, this sentiment can be through a loving word, a prayer, or just a presence. We all know that children have an inherent desire to be loved. But at night, it is just as imperative for them to understand that they are protected.

Because of this, many parents lead their children in a simple prayer before they close their eyes for the rest of the evening. Many of us are probably familiar with the nursery rhyme offered to God. The first line acknowledges that is time for rest. The second requests protection of the soul that is defenseless in the resting body. The third offers recognition of the possibility of not waking up again. And the last is a request that the Lord will take their soul to heaven. Though the rhyme offers a sentiment of innocence when recited by a child, it can come across as a rather dark prayer.

The prayer acknowledges the defenselessness of the sleeping body, but even more so the importance of the soul. Even from a young age, children understand that a person's body is secondary in its value compared to their soul. What does this have to do with peace? What does this have to do with being still before the Lord? Well, when we acknowledge the fact that our soul is that which is eternal, it is understandable to worry about its eternal placement. When our bodies lose their usefulness as the keeper of the soul, we want to know the final resting place of that soul. It is why we find peace in placing its safety in the hands of the Father. In His protection, we have nothing to fear. We can rest knowing that we will either wake to serve Him again or will rest in the loving arms of God.

HEAVENLY FATHER, I THANK YOU FOR PROTECTING ME IN THE MOMENTS WHERE I CANNOT PROTECT MYSELF. I THANK YOU FOR THE PEACE IN KNOWING THAT YOU ARE WITH ME EVEN IN THE MOMENTS WHERE I FIND REST. CONTINUE TO PROTECT ME, LORD, AND ALWAYS KNOW THAT MY WISH IS FOR YOU TO KEEP MY SOUL ALWAYS. AMEN.

54

LET'S JUST BE SAFE

*Do not be conformed to this age, but be transformed
by the renewing of your mind, so that you may discern
what is the good, pleasing, and perfect will of God.*

ROMANS 12:2

Alan has been an active athlete well into his late thirties. He played in just about every offering of a church-league sport. He exercised daily and maintained a healthy diet. On all accounts, it would appear that he was the model for holistic fitness. But a few weeks after his thirty-ninth birthday, he noticed there was a pull in his left calf. It caused minor discomfort, so he did not pay much attention to it. But after a month of running on it, the tug on his calf was starting to cause pain and not just discomfort. After a few more weeks, he was in excruciating pain whenever he exercised. It finally came to the point where his wife insisted that he go to the doctor "just to be safe." Alan had a feeling that it was just a pulled muscle, but respected the request of his wife and made an appointment.

When he finally arrived at the doctor's office, the doctor asked him to describe his routine. He said that he woke up early in the morning, drank a glass of water, and went for a five-mile run every morning. Then, in the afternoons, he would go to the gym and lift weights for about an hour and depending on the day, he would go and play basketball at his church for his men's league.

The doctor, admittedly impressed at his fitness regiment, asked about the pain itself. After he described the pain, he asked, "How much time do you spend stretching before and after you exercise?" Alan, now a little ashamed, looked down and acknowledged that he never really ever had to stretch. Offering a smile and a clap on Alan's back, the doctor said, "You're almost forty. You're in great shape, but you're not in your twenties anymore. If you want to continue exercising this way, you are going to have to learn how to stretch. So, go home. Ice your leg and take a week off from running and you should be fine."

Alan felt a tremendous relief over the news. Even though he was frustrated that he still had to pay for the visit, he was happy to do so, knowing that he now had the peace of taking in wisdom he could trust. For many of us, we forget the importance of seeking wisdom when we just don't feel right about a situation. We assume that certain circumstances will work themselves out. As Christians, however, we know the importance of a wise word from an elder, a respected colleague, or the Word of God. The next time you are dealing with a potential frustration, true wisdom is discovered by seeking a solution to something before it becomes a problem. Proactivity is important.

LORD, I KNOW THERE ARE TIMES WHEN I WANT TO ALLOW CERTAIN THINGS TO FALL WHERE THEY MAY. PLEASE REMIND ME OF THE IMPORTANCE OF SEEKING WISDOM, EVEN IF IT MEANS MY ISSUE IS NOT THAT SERIOUS. REMIND ME THAT PEACE IS DISCOVERED IN PROACTIVITY. AMEN.

55

PENCILS DOWN!

Whatever your hands find to do, do with all your strength, because there is no work, planning, knowledge, or wisdom in Sheol where you are going.

ECCLESIASTES 9:10

I doubt that there are any of us who have not heard the authoritarian call to let students know that the time for the test is finished. For many, even though the quiz is over, the apprehension over the upcoming grade is only beginning. All students stand at their desks, take their test sheets, and place them on their teacher's desk. Then, many students will lower their heads and accept a defeat before it has ever been confirmed. Now, to be fair, some students are correct in their assumptions. They did not study. They did not take the time to prepare for the quiz, or they did not pay attention when the teacher was reviewing the material. This is not a message for them. This message is for those that have turned in hard work and assumed that defeat was tied to its difficulty.

The reality is that many people struggle with this sentiment. We assume that difficult work means we were somehow not qualified to accomplish the task at hand. This perspective is devastating for those who seek to endeavor well. Many individuals will place the weight of defeat on their shoulders even if success is on the other side. This appearance can show up in a multitude of ways. A student prepares for a test and may do well. But if they feel that it was still difficult, then they must have failed to study with the correct amount of effort. A worker may turn in a project that is appreciated by all, but because she lost many nights of sleep, then there must have been someone more qualified to do the job.

The problem with this kind of perspective is that we cannot confuse the difficulty of one's work with one's ability to do the work in the first place. Some tasks are just going to be difficult. It is a reality that all of us will encounter. Just because a task is difficult does not mean that you are unqualified to do the job. Are there going to be jobs that need qualifications? Yes, of course. We do not want math teachers performing heart surgery! But just because you have two hundred legal pages to read does not mean that you are not a good lawyer. Just because you may have a day when you have to answer one hundred emails does not mean that you are a poor communicator.

Hard work is a reality for all of us. Tough seasons will arrive no matter who you are. But the arrival of frustration is not an indicator of your ability to take it on. God will not give you anything that you cannot handle without His help. We can take a breath and know that just because the work is hard does not mean that we are not a valuable worker.

GOD, I KNOW THERE HAVE BEEN MOMENTS WHEN I HAVE ASSUMED THAT BECAUSE THE WORK IS HARD, I MUST NOT BE ABLE TO TAKE ON THE RESPONSIBILITY OF DOING IT. PLEASE ALLOW ME TO TAKE A BREATH AND KNOW YOU HAVE CALLED ME TO PERFORM THE TASK AT HAND AND THAT EVEN THOUGH IT IS DIFFICULT, IT DOES NOT MEAN I SHOULD NOT DO IT. AMEN.

YOU CANNOT REST IN TENSION

*Let all bitterness, anger and wrath, shouting
and slander be removed from you, along with
all malice. And be kind and compassionate
to one another, forgiving one another, just
as God also forgave you in Christ.*

EPHESIANS 4:31–32

If there is anything the year 2020 showed, it is that many of us can stay in a form of stasis regarding potential tension with others. Regardless of your views on politics or lockdowns, we all had people we care for that we either avoided or withheld information from to keep the peace. It could probably be said, however, that keeping the peace is nowhere near the same as making peace. To keep the peace is to keep the status quo. The sentiment of this is simple. I may disagree with you, so instead of talking about our disagreements and seeking peace with each other, I will not say anything. After all, the absence of strife must be peace. Right? How wrong this mind-set is! Even though there may be no strife on the surface, that potential conflict is simmering under the surface. The person with whom you find frustration may not even be aware of your anger, but there is a boiling point that results in outrageous conflict or abandonment.

What do we do in the stress of this situation? We do our very best to rest in it. We assume that just because the surface is calm that there is nothing underneath that needs addressing. What does this do to friendships? Well, intimacy is lost. If I cannot share my thoughts on an important subject, our relationship will become more shallow. If we only discuss the things we agree on, then there is no depth to the relationship. The true depth of friendship roots itself in honesty. If I have to withhold honesty to protect the friendship, then the relationship is based on a lie. If I am hiding a part of who I am to avoid conflict and refuse to reveal an honest sentiment, I am only displaying a falsehood. This is no way to live, especially with other believers.

The cost of this behavior is anxiety, bitterness, and the worst kind of seclusion. Deception provides a wall of protection around our hearts, and more often than not, we protect a relationship that may not be worth having in the first place. After all, if there is no honesty in the friendship, is that person a friend, or are they just a conflict you are trying to avoid? There is no peace in this kind of behavior. There is no way to find a lasting relationship with someone who cannot receive your honesty. This does not mean to speak without grace, but it does mean if you are hiding from someone, then you are only masquerading as someone who cares when in reality, you are only avoiding that which may need to be confronted.

LORD, I KNOW I HAVE NOT SHOWN MY TRUE COLORS TO THE ONES I LOVE. I HAVE ACTED COWARDLY AND HID BEHIND THE GUISE OF NOT WANTING TO SEEK CONFLICT. GOD, GIVE ME THE COURAGE TO BE HONEST. AMEN.

DEMOLITION DAY

**Therefore, if anyone is in Christ, he is a new creation;
the old has passed away, and see, the new has come!**

2 CORINTHIANS 5:17

For Lauren, her soon-to-be dream house and her current home was the same. She loved her town. She adored her neighbors, but she lived in a home built in the 1970s and still had the green carpet in the bathroom to prove it. Her house was in desperate need of a face-lift. So, she packed up enough belongings to stay with her parents for a few months, moved into her old home, and hired a contractor. When discussing the project, she provided the contractor with two lists: a want list and a need list. Her list of wants was long and included things such as granite countertops, hardwood floors, updated tile in the bathrooms, and the like. On her list of needs, she wanted to convert one of the bedrooms to an office and wanted to knock down a wall to provide her home with a more open floor plan.

After the two went down the list and worked out a budget, Lauren found out that she would be able to get everything she was after within her budget if they made a few budget-minded changes. Nevertheless, she moved forward with the process. To clarify, Lauren is someone who has to know the plan. She does not feel comfortable with moving forward with something if she cannot see the path ahead. Because of this, it was not a shock when she started to panic when she came by the house on demolition day. Her counters were destroyed. She found holes in the wall. Parts of her floor were missing, and there was an unnerving amount of dust from broken drywall that filled the air.

When she approached the contractor, her frustration had brought her to a place of panic. She assumed that her home was broken and unable to be repaired. She could not understand why the process was so chaotic and was prepared to request a refund for the cost of his services. Now, the contractor was a wise man who had been in the business for a long time. He waited for her to finish her rant, and then said in a kind low voice, "Ma'am, in this business, you've got to make a mess of the old to bring about the new."

Lauren stopped for a moment; she knew that the process was going to take a bit of trust on her part, but she never fully realized that to have the new parts of the home, she had to allow the destruction of the old. The hardest part about the Christian faith is the acknowledgment that a new life demands the destruction of the old. We cannot have peace if we choose to hold onto both.

HEAVENLY FATHER, PLEASE ALLOW ME TO LET GO OF MY OLD WAYS SO I MAY KNOW YOU MORE. ALLOW ME TO REALIZE THAT FOR ME TO HAVE A NEW LIFE, I HAVE TO LET GO OF THE OLD. AMEN.

58

GOD'S WHISPER

Do not love the world or the things in
the world. If anyone loves the world, the
love of the Father is not in him.

1 JOHN 2:15

There is an exercise that is used in youth groups all over the country. The youth leader will take on the role of God to have a conversation with a student. While doing this, however, students and other leaders will act as distractions that pop up in the life of everything that could happen in a student's life. The youth leader will keep his voice low, but the distractions will keep their voices elevated. What does this do? Well, the most obvious lesson to be learned from the exercise is that distractions are loud. They do everything in their power to keep your attention away from what matters. The other lesson is that God is not one who fights for your attention. His desire may very well be to know and be known, but He does not need our worship.

While the exercise plays out, the leader will give messages that are easy to understand without distraction, but when in a room loaded with distraction, the messages become more and more difficult to remember. Even the students with exceptional listening abilities struggle with the exercise. The leader will say phrases like, "I need six blue eggs" or "I would like three orange rocking chairs and seven pink ones" or "Can you give me four purple crayons and two green ones?"

After the chaos settles, the leader asks the student for details about the messages in no particular order. The student soon realizes that even though the messages were relatively simple, he or she is unable to recall much of the information that has been given to them. Normally, students will play the game three or four times until someone finally learns the secret to the success of the game.

To win, a student must get close to the leader and listen intently to his words. Not only that but the student must also block out the distractions that would keep him from hearing the messages from the leader.

This exercise is something that we can apply in our own lives. There are plenty of distractions that pull us away from hearing what God wants us to hear, and the reality is that they do not have that much power over us. We might have work responsibilities or a family to support. But outside of that, the mountain of distractions in our lives does not have to be there. We have given it too much power and allowed it to overwhelm the still small voice that God uses to tell us that which is most important.

HEAVENLY FATHER, I KNOW THERE HAVE BEEN MOMENTS WHEN I HAVE ALLOWED DISTRACTIONS TO MAINTAIN MY FOCUS WHEN THEY SHOULD NOT. PLEASE REMIND ME OF YOUR GOODNESS AND REMIND ME TO LISTEN INTENTLY TO ALL THAT YOU WOULD HAVE ME HEAR. AMEN.

59

THE WAY THE DOMINOS FALL

**Our Lord is great, vast in power;
his understanding is infinite.**

PSALM 147:5

When Eric was a young boy, he loved playing with dominos. He was not a fan of playing the actual game of dominos. Instead, he would stack them in a sequence and allow them to fall, tilting one slightly only to cause the fall of the rest. One afternoon, while playing with his grandfather, he was asked if the first domino ever thinks its impact will affect the last. Eric was confused by his grandfather's question. "It's just a domino, Grandpa. It doesn't think about anything." His grandfather smiled, picked up a domino, and said, "Pretend it does. You have a long line of dominos. Does the one at the front of the line think about the one at the last?"

Eric thought for a moment and then said, "No, I don't think so."

"And why is that?" Eric's grandfather asked.

"Well, the first one is in this room, but the last one is in the next. There is no way it could know," Eric said, knowing that there must be a point to this line of questioning.

"If the last domino does not realize what the first domino has done, then why should the first domino fall at all?" Eric's grandfather asked again, wanting to challenge his grandson.

"This domino knocks down the first one. The next domino knocks down the next one, and the next one, and all the others . . . that's why it's important," Eric finally said, defending his practice of knocking over dominos.

Eric would realize in life that the effect we have on others matters in ways that we cannot even imagine. Eric, at the age of seven, simply wanted to knock down rectangular blocks, but this nugget of wisdom stuck with him as he grew older. At his grandfather's funeral, Eric realized the man had affected many lives other than his. Men and women discussed the lessons they learned from him and how they applied them to others. They pointed to how their children, coworkers, and church members had never met Eric's grandfather, but they had all heard his wisdom in one way or another.

Many times, we do not realize the kind of effect we will have on other people. We do not stop and think about the reality of a kind word that is shown to others and how that moment might affect others we will never come to know. And yet, that is how God works. Through His perfect foresight, He showed us all love and grace that would be shared with others. Some of you reading this can probably recall a person who affected you in incredible ways and how his or her example has been shown in your own life in the way you affect others. They may know the person who changed you, but they are all grateful for the way you have been changed by their example.

LORD, GOD, I THANK YOU FOR ALL YOU HAVE DONE BY PROVIDING WONDERFUL EXAMPLES IN MY LIFE. THERE ARE SO MANY I LOVE DEEPLY WHO DO NOT KNOW HOW I HAVE BEEN CHANGED BY THOSE WHO YOU HAVE PLACED IN MY LIFE. ALLOW ME TO BE THE CHANGE THAT AFFECTS THE FUTURE FOR YOUR GLORY AND YOUR KINGDOM. AMEN.

THE COMPLEXITY OF YOU

Let love be without hypocrisy.
Detest evil; cling to what is good.

ROMANS 12:9

Have you ever looked up to the sky at night and gazed upon the stars? When we are children, we can assume that they are specks of light used to pierce the darkness. But after reading about them in astronomy textbooks, we note that they are complex orbs of fire that burn for unimaginable amounts of time. This concept is the same with other sciences. When we observe biology and can witness the nature of a multicellular organism, we cannot help but notice the complexity of the cell itself. With physics, letting go of a ball and watching it hit the floor and bounce back to our hands is a natural occurrence. But ask any physicist, and he or she will be able to communicate complex laws of motion that explain any observable movement.

In the world of Christian thought, these kinds of observations center around the argument of God's existence called the "Finely Tuned Argument." Our world, from the laws of physics to cellular biology all point to a personal creation. From plants to animals and the laws of the world in which they live, many Christian scientists describe a "readability" to the known world. This is also the case with you.

Within every human being is a blueprint that points to the uniqueness of the individual that God has created you to be. By observing the strands of your DNA, scientists can understand your eye color, your hair color, or why you are tall or short. There are even indicators that point to minimal qualities, like whether or not you have freely swinging earlobes or have the ability to twist your tongue. God, the all-powerful creator of the universe, knows you down to the most infinitesimal details.

What does this have to do with stillness? Why should we feel peace from this knowledge? Well, when you approach God, you are standing before the Creator who knows you so intimately that you do not have to hide anything from Him. He knows how you think. He knows your characteristics as well as your flaws, and yet, He loves you anyway. You do not have to worry about putting on a Christian disguise before the Father. You can be who He created you to be. You were not created to be perfect. You were created to be made perfect.

God knows who you are. Do not worry about displaying some form of false worthiness, and just live authentically before Him. He will take care of the rest.

HEAVENLY FATHER, I THANK YOU FOR CREATING ME WITH ALL OF MY PERFECT IMPERFECTIONS. I THANK YOU FOR KNOWING ME SO INTIMATELY THAT I DO NOT HAVE TO BE ANYTHING OTHER THAN WHAT YOU HAVE CREATED ME TO BE. REMIND ME OF YOUR GOODNESS, YOUR WISDOM, AND YOUR LOVE. ALLOW ME TO SEEK AFTER IT EVERY DAY. AMEN.

SHUT OFF YOUR NOTIFICATIONS

**Let your eyes look forward; fix
your gaze straight ahead.**
PROVERBS 4:25

Y ou have made the halfway mark through this book. Congratulations on your dedication. You have shown a consistent discipline in taking the time to be still for at least five minutes out of your day and seeking ways to rest in God and not in the trivial pauses that the world may bring. Now, here is a more difficult question. How many of these little moments have been interrupted by a text message or an email? How many times have you taken the time to read through an entry in this book and could finish it without interruption? Chances are, if you are like most individuals, you have probably placed down this book and checked on the little ding that comes from your device.

We know that work can wait. We know that it will only take five minutes to say a quick prayer over that which is on our hearts. We understand the importance of taking a moment to stop and go to God with either thanksgiving or concern. Still, many of us can recall the countless moments when we have allowed the ways of the world to pull our gaze away from heaven. We do not want to admit it. If we are honest, there are even moments where we have pretended that the matter we are attending to is of the utmost urgency. Does this happen sometimes? Yes, of course. Are these urgent moments always as timely as we pretend they are? Well, that is between you and God.

We often confuse busyness with hard work. The ability to work long hours and answer emails outside of work can show dedication. But is that the thing to which we should be most dedicated? If work is what holds our attention the most, what comes second? If our responsibilities stand at the top spot of our priorities, where do other things fall? The harsh truth for today is that our hindrance to finding rest has very little to do with our work as much as our willingness to walk away from it. We may understand the sentiment behind this, but how many of us are willing to live up to it? Can that email wait? Do you have to answer that call right this second? Coming before God is not a task that is to be taken casually. We do not stand before the Father and put Him on hold when distractions fall in our lap. Peace is not only the arrival of stillness. It is an avoidance of that which keeps our minds moving.

HEAVENLY FATHER, I KNOW THERE HAVE BEEN TIMES WHEN I HAVE PLACED YOU SECOND WHEN I KNOW YOU SHOULD HAVE BEEN FIRST. I ASK FOR YOUR FORGIVENESS IN THIS. REMIND ME THAT BEING STILL MEANS NOT ONLY GOING AFTER YOU BUT LEAVING BEHIND THE THINGS THAT KEEP YOU FROM MY FOCUS. AMEN.

62

THE STACK OF BOOKS BY THE BED

Let me experience your faithful love in the morning, for I trust in you. Reveal to me the way I should go because I appeal to you.

PSALM 143:8

In nearly every household, we have at least one member that considers themselves to be a reader. We find little identifiers of this tendency throughout the home. You may find a bookshelf, a room dedicated to reading, or most likely, a stack of books next to the bed. Now, there are two possibilities for this stack's existence. The reader probably collects books at a pace that outruns their ability to read the books they already have, or this person may tend to collect books and not section off the amount of time needed to read them. It may take them a week or so to read a book if they give a couple of hours to each time slotted for reading, but they may get to bed late in the evening. And by the time they start reading, their mind is tired. Their body is ready for rest, and sleep only comes faster when they start reading.

Those needed two hours are only greeted by twenty to thirty minutes before the diligent mind collapses into unconsciousness. For the spouses, it is a comical sight to find their partner with a book on his or her face. The reader in the home will have made little progress and eventually find them behind schedule in their reading goals. And for the rest of the story, we know what happens. The stack of books gets just a little higher. The book we were so dedicated to reading has started to collect dust, and the charm of the sleeper reader has dissipated.

The reality is that the stack could be replaced with other things in our walk. Maybe you have just allowed the day to get away from you and have not made the time to pray to God. Is this okay? You will finish the day with the Lord, after all. What a beautiful sentiment! Right? Maybe reading the Word has become a priority, but somehow the days have been so busy that you have decided to do it before going to sleep.

It may seem thoughtful on paper, but think about what we are presenting when we go to God in this manner. We are not coming to Him with fresh eyes that are yearning for a fruitful encounter. We are making sure that we check the last box for the day.

I am not saying that we should not spend time with the Father before we sleep. We should go to Him in both the morning and in the evening. God, of course, should see us before we go to sleep. But even more so, He should see us when we rise and are ready to move forward with Him before our day ever gets started. We must prepare our feet and take a breath before moving, and the peace before we take our first step and after we take our last all rides on Him.

LORD, I KNOW THERE HAVE BEEN MOMENTS WHERE YOU HAVE BEEN THE LAST PRIORITY FOR THE DAY. KEEP ME FROM DOING THIS IN THE FUTURE AND REMIND ME TO START AND FINISH MY DAY WITH YOU. AMEN.

MY DIGITAL ASSISTANT

My son, if you accept my words and store up
my commands within you, listening closely to
wisdom and directing your heart to understanding;
furthermore, if you call out to insight and lift
your voice to understanding, if you seek it like
silver and search for it like hidden treasure,
then you will understand the fear of the LORD
and discover the knowledge of God.

PROVERBS 2:1–5

I often go to my digital assistant when I need questions answered. "How hot should the oven be for chocolate chip cookies?" "What store has the best deal for an air fryer?" "Can you remind me to take out the dog this afternoon?" "How long is the Great Wall of China?" "What is the difference between a white-tie and a black-tie event?" There are countless questions that I have asked my digital assistant, but they are frequently of a specific kind. I do not ask questions like, "Where do I find peace?" or "How can I improve my prayer life?" I know that somewhere on the Internet, someone has written a blog that will give me some information that may be helpful on the practical level, but it will probably only give me advice I already know.

In reality, I know there is only one person I can go to who can give me the sense of peace I could never discover on my own. My digital assistant may be helpful when it comes my day-to-day tasks. Honestly, I do not know where I would be without my phone reminding me to do something that would slip through the cracks. I am not sure how many teaspoons are in a tablespoon. I may need a recipe that assists me in making a chocolate chess pie. I am not sure what the Spanish word for pencil is. My phone is useful in many ways, but its usefulness in the minor should never be confused with that which is major.

One of the greatest mistakes we as Christians have made is the confusion of knowledge for wisdom. Wisdom comes from seeking God. When I come before the Father seeking answers, I do not waste His time asking for recipes, measurements, or translations. I go to Him with a yearning to know Him more. I fall on my knees in humility to ask for guidance in frustrating situations, in celebrations, and during seasons of sadness.

God is all-knowing. He knows everything there is to know. So, can He tell you everything that a digital assistant can? Yes, of course, but think of how silly that would be to go ask God for directions to the grocery store. Instead, take the time to ask for direction over your life and see what difference His presence will make.

HEAVENLY FATHER, I ADMIT THERE ARE DAYS I WISH YOU WERE LIKE MY PHONE. I WISH THERE WERE TIMES WHEN YOU WOULD JUST GIVE ME THE ANSWER I AM SEEKING. REMIND ME THAT THE ONLY WAY TO DISCOVER TRUE WISDOM IS THROUGH MY KNOWLEDGE OF YOU. ALLOW ME TO DIG DEEPER INTO MY RELATIONSHIP WITH YOU AND REMIND ME TO REST IN YOU EACH DAY. AMEN.

64

CITY SUNRISE

"Stop fighting, and know that I am God, exalted
among the nations, exalted on the earth."

PSALM 46:10

Cities are most known for their nightlife. People are alive and well even into the early morning, but there is a unique calm that comes over the city when the sun begins to peek over the horizon. In the early hours of the morning, thousands of people have returned to their apartments and prepared for bed. The chaos of the night has ceased, and the burgundy glow of the sun starts filling the early morning sky. Stars are still visible, the moon is still shining, but instead of sounds of laughter, car engines, or busses in transit, you may hear something unexpected: birds.

From the birds' chirping, you may hear the subtle slap of tennis shoes hitting the pavement as early-morning runners greet the day. From the runners, you may notice apartment doors shut as early risers prepare to go to work. It is almost eerie. In a city marked by nonstop action, it is always strange to witness a couple of hours of silence where the metropolis rests between the disappearance of stars and rising of the sun.

It is interesting from that silence we can hear sounds that are lost in the chaos of all the other noise. The same can be noticed in Christianity. We can have worship services that resemble concerts. We can have sermons that sound more like motivational speeches, and we can have a building that can double as an event hall. With all of these bells and whistles, however, we can lose what God would have for us to hear. It is one of the many reasons that we are told to go off into a quiet place to spend time with the Lord. It is why we often hear that God speaks to us in a still, small voice.

Sometimes, the reason we cannot hear that which God has for us is that we are caught up in the chaos of the day-to-day. We miss what God has for us not because He is not speaking to us, but because we have put ourselves in a place where we cannot hear Him. So, the sun sets on our chaos. Allow for the quiet to come and realize that what God may have for us requires us to be quiet enough to hear it.

LORD, I KNOW THERE ARE TIMES WHERE I FEEL LOST AND FEEL I COULD NOT HEAR YOU. I APOLOGIZE BECAUSE I HAVE NEVER THOUGHT THAT MAYBE THE REASON I CANNOT HEAR FROM YOU IS BECAUSE MY WORLD IS SO LOUD. REMIND ME TO QUIET MY LIFE. ALLOW THE DISTRACTIONS OF MY DAY-TO-DAY TO SETTLE SO I CAN BE STILL AND LISTEN FOR THE THINGS YOU WOULD HAVE ME HEAR. CAUSE ME TO BE QUIET AND FIND PEACE IN ALL YOU WISH TO SAY TO ME. AMEN.

65

SHEET MUSIC

**I have treasured your word in my heart
so that I may not sin against you.**

PSALM 119:11

If you have some musical training, there is a strong possibility that you know how to read music. For some, they may be able to sight-read while the music is playing. Others may be able to find their note easily. But for those who compose music, there is a special joy that comes from knowing how to hear the notes that aren't played.

One violin player showed this skill as he was on his way to his first rehearsal for a piece that a friend of his had written. While on the bus to the orchestra, passersby would stare at the man as he nodded along to a song no one could hear. They watched the man in silence weave with sounds that did not exist yet. To those who had no musical training, I am sure he looked ridiculous. But for those who knew just enough music to know what was happening, they observed with slight envy. They were witnessing a man who knew the sounds before they came from an instrument.

As the violin player continued to bob along with the unplayed music, a little girl dared to approach the man and ask what he was doing. The violin player said, "I'm listening to music."

The little girl questioned him, "But where are your headphones?"

This brought a smile to the musician. He shared the view of his sheet music with the little girl and asked, "What do you see on this paper?"

She tilted her head this way and that, and finally, with a voice of exasperation, "It's just a bunch of dots."

The musician laughed and said, "When I was your age, I thought the same thing, too. But the more I learned about how to read these dots, the more I realized that they were telling me something more. They were singing a song to me."

The little girl, sensing a secret, said, "I want to hear them sing!"

With that, he pulled his violin from his case. He asked the little girl to point at a dot. When she did, he played the note. When she pointed to the next, he played that as well. Then, after she was satisfied, she dragged her finger along the sheet music as if she was reading a language she had not yet learned, and the musician played the song that he heard on his own without playing the first note.

You may have noticed a similar attitude regarding the Bible. Many people assume that it is only a two-thousand-year-old document with wisdom on how a person should or should not live. That is just not the case. There is a wealth of information displaying the love of God for His children. And yet, many do not take the time to pick up and study its message because they assume they know all there is to know about it.

HEAVENLY FATHER, FORGIVE ME FOR THE MOMENTS WHEN I HAVE TREATED THE BIBLE AS ANYTHING LESS THAN YOUR MESSAGE TO HUMANITY. PUT IN ME A HEART THAT DESIRES TO KNOW MORE AND MORE OF YOUR WORD. AMEN.

66

A FEW DEEP BREATHS

Yet the righteous person will hold to his way, and the one whose hands are clean will grow stronger.

JOB 17:9

There is a moment before every competition that leads up to the starting motion. Athletes will gather on the mat, the starting line, or the court and take a few deep breaths. Depending on the sport, before an athlete will take their first step, they do their best to calm their heart before taking on explosive activity. There is a reason behind this. If an athlete is going to compete well, they will have to be willing to slow their heart rate before going into the activity.

If you have ever played a sport, you are probably aware of what I am describing. A golfer will rarely find success in his swing if he does not calm down at the tee. A fighter with heightened nerves will have difficulty remaining calm in the ring, and a long-distance runner cannot run long if their heart is already beating through their chest when they approach the starting line. The ones who take on an obstacle with confidence and calmness are the ones who do not falter.

There is a similar happening in the Christian faith. The reality is that we live in a world marked by difficulty and frustration. It is inescapable. No matter the level of faith one has, obstacles, hindrances, and pitfalls are inevitable in this life. So, how are we to respond? How are we to deal with these moments we all will have to incur? The answer is the same, no matter the situation. Be still; go to God in prayer; take a few deep breaths; and step forward.

Our willingness to step forward does not come from our tenacity or stubbornness. It comes from our trust that God is amid our decision making. We believe that God has given us discernment in the moments when wisdom is needed. We must remember that as people who God has called to run the long race and to take up our crosses daily, we have not been asked to take something lightly. Some moments will seem daunting. Do not look at these moments through the lens of defeat. Look at them as opportunities to rely on God.

So, when you approach the starting line of the long race or stand before the mountain few are called to climb, do not focus on the frustration of having to take on the difficulties. Be still. Go to God. Take a few deep breaths, and start moving forward.

HEAVENLY FATHER, I KNOW THERE HAVE BEEN TIMES WHEN I HAVE ALLOWED THE DIFFICULT MOMENTS TO HINDER ME FROM RELYING ON YOU. I HAVE ASSUMED THAT THE PROBLEMS ARE TOO BIG FOR YOU TO HANDLE. ALLOW ME TO TAKE A BREATH AND TRUST THAT YOU ARE WITH ME IN BOTH THE EASY MOMENTS AS WELL AS THE DIFFICULT ONES. REMIND ME TO LIVE IN THIS TRUTH AND GIVE ME A HEART THAT SEEKS YOU IN THE EASY TIMES AS WELL AS THE HARD. AMEN.

67

THE THINKING MAN

Set your minds on things above, not on earthly things.
COLOSSIANS 3:2

The Thinker is a French sculpture that captures a man sitting on a rock and resting his chin on his fist to symbolize the depth of the thoughts that have him in place. You have likely seen replicas of the statue in museums or parks. But all in all, the action of the sculpture is meant to capture the notion of contemplation. The sculpture's origins are marked with allusions to *The Divine Comedy* by Dante Alighieri, but this is not our focus. What is notable about this sculpture is that it is a figure that always stands alone. Even when surrounded by chaos, we find separation from the chaotic nature of the world. Instead, we witness the calm state of a mind in thought.

There has been much discussion regarding the purpose of the sculpture over the years. Some observations are as innocent as speculating that the man is thinking on that which is perplexing. Maybe he is only thinking about why the grass is green or why the sky is blue. Others have darker speculations. According to a more depressing view, "the thinker" should be called "the regretter." He is not a man who ponders on why things are the way they are. Instead, they see a man who fixates on that which he could have done differently.

Whatever his state of mind may be, there is the shared observation that "the thinker" is one who is locked in thought. The debate is whether or not this thought is a curse or a blessing. But whatever the case, it should be stated that for "the thinker" to be completely locked in thought, he needs to block out the surrounding distractions. It does not matter what is happening around him. He is dedicated to his thoughts, and nothing will keep him from entertaining all the perplexities that come to him.

As Christians, many distractions pull our attention away from the Father. We have responsibilities at work, home, church, and plenty of other places. We have handheld devices that grab our attention and rarely refuse to let them go. A sign of a deep relationship with the Lord is one's ability to maintain a focus on that relationship. Does it mean that we sometimes have certain obligations come up that we cannot avoid? Of course! We, however, are called to know God and make Him known. We cannot expect success in this venture if we are not focused. Take time today to regain focus on that relationship. Feel free to rest your head on your chin and give it some thought. You may just be surprised what a little bit of focus can do for your relationship with God.

HEAVENLY FATHER, I KNOW I HAVE LOST MY FOCUS ON YOU. I KNOW THERE HAVE BEEN DAYS WHEN I HAVE NOT BEEN ABLE TO TAKE TIME WITH YOU. ALLOW ME TO REGAIN THAT FOCUS. AMEN.

68

HUMILITY IS QUIET

So, whether you eat or drink, or whatever you
do, do everything for the glory of God.

1 CORINTHIANS 10:31

We have all heard of the concept of the "humble brag." Someone will do something worthy of note and will decide to inform others of their accomplishments with a humble tone. In one regard, they will say, "Look what I have done." And in the next sentence, one may hear, "But it is not a big deal." My problem with this, of course, is that if something is not important to the person notifying me of their accomplishments, then they would not have announced it in the first place. Humility does not hide success or victory, but at the same time, it does not see the need in presenting it either.

Few people carry this example like Chris. He is a new deacon in a small church in the southern part of Mississippi. He serves on just about every committee. He went to seminary, and he even worked for a few years in the ministry. All of these are incredible qualities, and to find them in a deacon is something to be celebrated. However, the reason so many know of these qualities is because Chris finds a way to broadcast them. During meetings, he will find a way to say the phrase "When I was in seminary . . ." Or when he is assisting others, he's never afraid to talk about how he did the same sorts of things when he was a minister. This kind of behavior was charming at first. After all, who would not want a seminary-trained deacon who also has experience working for a church?

It was after a year, however, that Chris started to notice something. People did not seem to listen when he spoke. Their attention did not seem to change when Chris mentioned his experience and education. Chris, whether he liked it or not, found that people were no longer impressed. Dejected, he started becoming quieter. He did not speak up as much. Finally, after a few weeks, the chairman of the deacons asked Chris to stay after one of the meetings. Chris, assuming he was in trouble, did not know what to do in the situation.

The older deacon grinned a bit and asked if he could think of any deacons off the top of his head from his childhood. After pondering a bit, he realized that the only ones he could remember were either those who have given years and years of their lives to the service or those who were known for the worst reasons. After a few seconds of quiet, the chairman asked Chris, "Do you remember anything in particular that any one of them did?"

Chris pondered for a moment and said, "No, I can't."

The older man chuckled a bit and said, "And yet, you knew them as some of the best. Those who are more focused on doing God's will do amazing things and do not seem to care about being recognized for their works as long as God is the one who gets the glory."

LORD, I KNOW THERE HAVE BEEN TIMES WHEN I HAVE FORGOTTEN WHO IS SUPPOSED TO GET THE GLORY. PLEASE REMIND ME THAT MY WORK IN THIS LIFE IS TO BRING GLORY TO YOU. AMEN.

69

THE PAUSE
BEFORE PRAYER

**A time to tear and a time to sew; a time
to be silent and a time to speak.**

ECCLESIASTES 3:7

In a small rural community, there is a church that takes prayer seriously. Now, all churches have this claim, and all of them should. However, this little church shows their reverence for prayer in the way they enter into it. When the pastor prays over the congregation, he becomes still. He says, "Lord," and then remains silent for a few seconds. This practice, after years in ministry, has become intentional. When he was a young pastor, he did this to find the right words before diving into his time with God. Now, with more than thirty years of experience, he has reflected on the importance of coming to God with silence and appreciation before he ever utters a word.

According to this pastor, the most important thing a person can do during a worship service is pray. He desires to hear his congregants sing out to God and hopes they will listen to his sermon. But if he could only ask them to do one thing, he desperately desires for them to pray and to do it reverently.

When asked about this, he said, "I was a youth minister. I watched students fumble words, lose track of their thoughts, and show a relative uninterest in their prayers. When I was young, I did the same. But the more I came to know the

Lord, the more I realized that I am talking to the Creator. Does that not deserve a little bit of respect? So, I started challenging my students and said that we would call out to God and then pause for five seconds before speaking our next word."

After a few weeks of this, the pastor started noticing his students were taking their time in prayer more seriously. They would say "God" or "Lord" or "Father." They would then take a few moments, and then they would say whatever words came with their prayer. Their prayers had fewer "umms" or "uhhs." They sounded more eloquent and thoughtful. He allowed a few more weeks to pass with this exercise until he finally asked one of his students why they thought there was such a drastic change. A young girl responded to the question with a simple, but powerful answer, "When you think more about who you are talking to, you think more about what you are going to say."

The next time you go to God in prayer, take a moment. Be still, and think about who it is you are speaking with. You may notice that your prayers take on a sweeter, more loving, and more respectful tone because you have taken the time to be still before the Lord.

HEAVENLY FATHER, I ADMIT I HAVE NOT ALWAYS COME TO YOU WITH A REVERENT SPIRIT. I HAVE TRIED TO SQUEEZE IN A QUICK CONVERSATION BEFORE GOING TO BED, EATING A MEAL, OR DRIVING TO WORK. REMIND ME OF YOUR AUTHORITY AND POWER SO I MAY COME TO YOU WITH AWE AND RESPECT. AMEN.

70

PAUSE BEFORE YOU POST

The one who has knowledge restrains his words, and one who keeps a cool head is a person of understanding. Even a fool is considered wise when he keeps silent—discerning, when he seals his lips.

PROVERBS 17:27–28

If the year 2020 has taught us anything, we have probably relied too heavily on social media. Facebook, which was once a platform for graduates to keep in touch with old friends, has now become a cesspool of political debate and disparaging remarks on another person's beliefs. Instagram, designed to capture beautiful images on one's page, is now the primary home for Internet bullying. And as for Twitter, it started as a place for people to share snappy thoughts that would either amuse or challenge. Now, we find topics where opposing views are at war. People have lost the ability to think about how their comments may affect another person because we have lost the ability to have face-to-face conversations.

Now, to be clear, 2020 was not solely responsible for this occurrence. Many of us have either lost our job or had to change how we do it drastically. Very few places of work were able to carry on without change. Many went from offices and desks to homes and kitchen tables. We moved from having conversations around the water cooler and walking by desks to popping in on video chats and commenting on posts. This shift in communication moved from being personal to digital. We all noticed the difference. But still, we tried to trick ourselves into believing that this kind of interaction was almost just as good. Then, two weeks turned into two months. Two months turned into four. We viewed the news with hopes of hearing a hopeful word on a return to normalcy. When the television did not tell us enough, we started gleaning more and more from social media. And then, we started sharing our opinions.

I am not saying that we should not share our opinions, but sometimes I fear we may confuse lacking tact for a bold thought. But the more we shared our ideas, the more we were invested in them being right. Then, somewhere along the line, we no longer viewed dissenting opinion as a challenging thought. We viewed an honest debate with dissent and anger toward the person who challenged us. We observed disagreement as treason and the ones who carried the challenge as traitors to our relationship.

Online tension removed our ability to have discussions, and eventually, our ability to pause before we post. Whether you are right or wrong in your assumptions, you must remember that there is a person behind the profile. Think about the way you are commenting on someone's post. If you disagree, are you commenting with grace? Are you treating them with kindness? Or do you maybe need to think about whether or not you should post at all?

LORD, I KNOW THERE HAVE BEEN MOMENTS IN THE PAST WHERE I HAVE BEEN ZEALOUS IN THE WORST WAYS. WHETHER I AM RIGHT OR WRONG IS NOT THE ISSUE SO MUCH AS IT IS HOW I HAVE TREATED PEOPLE YOU HAVE PLACED IN MY LIFE. PLEASE REMIND ME TO HOLD MY TONGUE, AND REST IN YOUR GRACE. AMEN.

71

THE PEACE IN SEEKING WISDOM

For wisdom is better than jewels, and nothing desirable can equal it. I, wisdom, share a home with shrewdness and have knowledge and discretion.

PROVERBS 8:11–12

Some people do not enjoy the process of learning. For some, they may not have a hungry mind. They do not have a natural curiosity that drives them to learn. For most, however, a time constraint hinders the learning process. Maybe they have too much on their plate, or they have too many responsibilities, or they do not have enough time in the day. Whatever the case may be, there is a deep need for us to not only have wisdom but to seek it.

When someone does not have wisdom, certain situations become a little more arduous to handle. We lack tact in confronting conflict. We miss opportunities to learn from someone who has lived more life than we have. We miss out on moments of humility. Our understanding of others seems to be constrained. There is an obvious benefit to wisdom, but how do we know we have found it?

Well, by God's providence, Christians have the Bible as the ultimate tool for seeking wisdom. Pastors, apologists, and theologians may have collectively written hundreds of thousands of pages over a lifetime regarding Scripture. But if they are worth their salt as teachers, they will all agree that the foundation of their writings is the Word of God. There is peace in that. Sure, we may know many people of intellect who teach on the Bible, but the ones people seek out the most are the ones who are marked with humility. We do not seek arrogance. We may find a flare to the teachings of a confident pastor, but we are never shocked when we find out that profound teaching comes from the one who hides behind the cross.

When we seek wisdom, look for a quiet humility first. Boldness in the faith comes to those who are also quiet by nature. Those who possess this quiet humility often hold the most profound nuggets of wisdom. They are not people who flaunt their intellect, or the lessons God has taught them. Instead, the most remarkable teachers are the ones who point to others who taught them the most important lessons. When you find these people, you normally do not have to question whether or not you have discovered someone special. These people, in their silence, carry a peace that they share with those they teach. This peace has two characteristics. For one, the way these people discuss topics will be done with grace. And for the other, these people will often point others to the God who has provided the wisdom they are willing to share.

HEAVENLY FATHER, I KNOW I NEED TO LEARN MORE ABOUT YOU. I KNOW THE FIRST PLACE I SHOULD START IS YOUR WORD. PLEASE REMIND ME TO DIG DEEPER INTO THE BIBLE AND PROVIDE ME WITH A PERSON WHO CAN SHARPEN ME AND SHOW ME HOW TO SEEK WISDOM. AMEN.

CRUSHED BY ANXIETY

"Come to me, all of you who are weary and
burdened, and I will give you rest. Take up my
yoke and learn from me, because I am lowly and
humble in heart, and you will find rest for your
souls. For my yoke is easy and my burden is light."

MATTHEW 11:28–30

Anxiety comes for us all. It does not matter if we are calm under pressure. It does not only come to those who need mental preparation for any and every occasion. Anxiety is something that all of us will have to deal with on some level. The increase of the medicated population is an obvious indicator of the issue of anxiety in our society. The reality is that many of us have forgotten what to do in the face of fear. Many have forgotten how to quiet our souls before we take the first step in quieting our minds. Even if we finally find stillness in our bodies, our mind races with thoughts that cause apprehension and frustration. One of the best descriptions of this kind of mind-set came from a patient of a clinical psychologist.

As she lay on the couch, rubbing the tops of her hands, she finally concluded that her anxiety was like a rock that was just heavy enough for her to hold, but not enough to move as quickly as the rest of the world. As she carried this weight, some would walk past her seeming to be as light as a feather. They seemed to not carry any weight at all. For others, she would notice that they were slower. She could acknowledge that they had their weight to carry. But for some reason, they seemed to be moving just fine. According to her observation, some people were lucky enough to not have to carry anything, but the rest who did have a weight seemed to handle it with relative ease. That was the most crushing feeling. It was not that other people had no burden to carry. She was happy for them. Her depression and anxiety came from those who seemed to have issues of their own but were managing them well. The only conclusion must be that something was wrong with her.

As the psychologist finished scribbling notes on her paper, she looked up to her patient with understanding eyes. When the girl wrapped up the last of her frustrations, the psychologist asked, "Why do you think the people with burdens carry them better than you?"

For a moment, the girl thought deeply about that question. She had put so much focus on herself that she never thought about why the other people seemed to have a better handle of their burdens. She only fixated on what was wrong with her and not what was right with others. After a few more seconds of silence, she threw out a guess, "Either their burdens are lighter than mine, or someone has given them the strength to carry them."

DEAR GOD, MY HEART IS HEAVY. I NEED YOU. PLEASE TAKE THE BURDENS THAT I DEAL WITH EACH DAY FROM MY SHOULDERS AND ALLOW ME TO FOLLOW THE PATH YOU HAVE SET BEFORE ME. AMEN.

73

KNOWN BY FRUIT

"You'll recognize them by their fruit. Are grapes
gathered from thornbushes or figs from thistles?
In the same way, every good tree produces good
fruit, but a bad tree produces bad fruit. A good
tree can't produce bad fruit; neither can a bad
tree produce good fruit. Every tree that doesn't
produce good fruit is cut down and thrown into
the fire. So you'll recognize them by their fruit."

MATTHEW 7:16–20

We must never forget the reality of God's existence in our lives. It is one thing to note that God exists. It is another thing entirely to recognize God's presence in our lives. God's love for us is something that can be observed in our daily walk. If that is the case, we can live in the tremendous peace of knowing that God is with us.

Many of us do not know what to think of this. We do not know how to observe whether God is alive and well in the lives of those who claim to know Him. It should be stated that this is not an invitation to arbitrarily judge whether or not God is present in the lives of other believers, but there are a few indicators that help us identify other believers without them having to tell us.

The most notable one is by our fruit. If you have ever sat in church more than once, you probably have a little familiarity with the notion of fruit. If we see a healthy branch, we are not shocked to find a good fruit hanging from it. If we see one that is decaying, we find a fruit that matches the branch. We, however, never find a ripe, healthy fruit hanging from a dying branch. And if we see a seemingly healthy branch that produces bad fruit, it is likely sick and should be cut off before it infects the rest of the tree.

This illustration found in the book of Matthew points to the warning of those who pretend to be Christians. These are people who know just enough of the Bible to get them in trouble. You may see them in church every Sunday. They may be able to pray eloquently, and they may even be known to volunteer regularly. But it should be noted that these are all actions. It will be described later in the book of Galatians what the fruits of the Spirit are. These fruits do not indicate action as much as they indicate how we act. God is not interested in our works as much as He is interested in the heart behind the works. There is a peace in that. We do not have to do the right things. We simply have to be willing to have a certain heart that points to God in whatever we do. That may sound daunting, but the more we think on that prospect, the more grace that we discover.

HEAVENLY FATHER, I THANK YOU FOR THE LOVE YOU HAVE SHOWN ME IN ALL THAT YOU HAVE DONE. SHAPE MY HEART, LORD, IN A WAY THAT BRINGS GLORY TO YOU. AMEN.

74

REASSURED
BY GOD

Love is patient, love is kind. Love does not envy, is
not boastful, is not arrogant, is not rude, is not self-
seeking, is not irritable, and does not keep a record
of wrongs. Love finds no joy in unrighteousness but
rejoices in the truth. It bears all things, believes
all things, hopes all things, endures all things.

1 CORINTHIANS 13:4–7

We all seek reassurance. In our jobs, we want to know that we are doing good work and that our employment is secure. We desire to know that the money we are making is enough to take care of the needs of our loved ones. With our family, we need to know we are loved and that the people we care for know we love them. With our goals, we need to know they are measurable and able to be accomplished. Even with our salvation, we can have moments when we reach out to God to make sure that we are still His child.

Reassurance is a part of the human experience, but there is no greater need for reassurance then being loved. When we are young children, we go to our parents and seek to be carried, held, or played with. When we are teenagers, we look up to the seats to see if our parents are watching us because we want to make them proud. When we finish our education, we likely look to those who have been there for us throughout our lives. When we fall in love, we look for opportunities to show affection to our potential spouse and hope that attention is reciprocated. And as we dive deeper into our faith, we have probably had a crisis where we go to God just to make sure that He still loves us.

Think about the moments when you have gone to God like this. We do not do this when we think about how lovable we are. We often go to God with this kind of attitude when life has been difficult. We go to Him seeking this kind of reassurance when we have acted in a way that we know does not glorify Him, and like a child who has just broken a precious item, we stand before the Father seeking forgiveness. We, however, do not only seek forgiveness at this moment. We want to know that He still loves us even though we have acted against Him.

It is good to find remorse, regret, and guilt in the moments when we have done something wrong. We should feel a twist in our hearts when we do that which we know we should not, but we should also know that God does not keep tabs on His children because that is not the nature of His love. He has forgiven you for sins that you have not even committed yet. God loves you despite your sin. God loves you because He has removed the thing He cannot stand from you. You are not perfect, but God will make you perfect by removing your sin. In that, we find reassurance in knowing that God's love is not something that falls in the face of a bad decision.

HEAVENLY FATHER, THANK YOU FOR LOVING ME. I KNOW I DO NOT DESERVE IT, AND THE FACT THAT YOU LOVE ME DESPITE MY INABILITY TO BE PERFECT AS YOU ARE PERFECT GIVES ME A SENSE OF GRACE I CAN NEVER REPAY. AMEN.

HE IS UP TO SOMETHING GOOD

Trust in the LORD with all your heart, and do not rely on your own understanding; in all your ways know him, and he will make your paths straight.

PROVERBS 3:5–6

Doris always found a way to place a phrase in her prayers. She would often say, "You are up to something good." You could never predict exactly where it would be in her prayers, but you always knew that it would find its place somewhere in it. She would say it at the dinner table. She would say it while kneeling next to her bed. She said it while praying over her grandchildren, and she would always say it at church if the pastor asked her to pray. She was the definition of a prayer warrior.

After years and years of studying Scripture, serving her church, and going on the mission field, thousands of people had heard the phrase, "You are up to something good." According to Doris, she had never found anything in the Bible that made her think otherwise. Even when there was turmoil on the horizon, there was always the promise of joy and peace on the other side. When Egypt enslaved the Israelites, there was freedom on the other side. When the Israelites wandered in the wilderness, the promised land was on the horizon.

When mankind was trapped by sin, God sent His Son. And when Jesus died on the cross, there was life on the third day.

Doris was a woman of unshakable faith. She was raised in the Great Depression. She worked in a factory during World War II, and she grew up never knowing wealth. And yet, joy and peace were part of her daily demeanor. She did not understand how anyone who loved the Lord could not constantly see His goodness in the daily lives of Christians.

This attitude did not mean she was ignorant. Her heart still broke for those who went to bed hungry. She was bothered when she witnessed injustice, and she always helped those who were in need, but when she looked in the eyes of the people she helped she always did the same thing no matter the person. She prayed. She held the hands of those who were hurting and prayed over their circumstance. During the prayer, she would say her little phrase, and when the prayer was over, she would continue holding the hands of the person and in a soft, but bold, voice, she would say, "He *is* up to something good."

This phrase never lost its truth, but it provided peace for the ones who heard it. Whatever your circumstances are today, know that God is with you and that He is up to something good.

HEAVENLY FATHER, I KNOW THERE HAVE BEEN TIMES WHEN I HAVE NOT TRUSTED IN YOU. I HAVE NOT TRUSTED THAT MY CIRCUMSTANCES ARE A PART OF YOUR PLAN. ALLOW ME TO HAVE FAITH IN YOUR GOODNESS AND ALLOW ME TO TRUST THAT YOU ARE UP TO SOMETHING GOOD. AMEN.

CARING FOR SOMEONE THROUGH THEIR WORK

"Because I, the LORD, have not changed, you
descendants of Jacob have not been destroyed."

MALACHI 3:6

Every company has its way of operating, and many companies with over fifty employees have many moving parts. It is because of this built-in chaos that there is often a recognition of the work that is being done well within the company. Sometimes there will be an award. Other times an employee might find a raise or bonus attached to their check. Sometimes, it can be something as simple as a manager ordering some sweets to celebrate the success of one of their employees. How it is done is not as important as the general act of recognizing work in the first place.

In one company, there is a boss who takes special care to recognize good work when he hears about it. He always takes time to honor the team member who has provided good work to the team. Even though he only has fifteen people on his team, they are all a dedicated bunch who enjoy working together. After a few years, however, this boss started to notice that his recognition was settling on the same five or six people who were on his team. He knew his team was exemplary and that all of them did good work, but he could not understand why he was celebrating the same five or six people.

He decided to do a bit of thinking on the topic. He worked for a major newspaper on the editorial team, so he felt confident he could figure out the issue. After a few hours, he noticed three employees who he had never recognized in the seven years he had been the boss. At first, his immediate inclination was that they must not be doing good work. But the more he thought about it, the more he realized the nature of the jobs of the three people who were working under him. One of them was a woman named Megan.

Megan had been a part of the newspaper ever since they started taking their publication online. She was in charge of data entry. She spent hours playing with algorithms and spreadsheets that would allow her to track the traffic coming to the website. She also researched best practices to get more eyes to the website. By the very nature of her job, if you noticed nothing was wrong with the website, then that meant she was doing her job well.

The manager had never given it this much thought before. He assumed the moments we do our jobs well are the moments where we shine, but sometimes, good work is shown so often that we can forget about the level of its goodness.

LORD, I ADMIT THERE HAVE BEEN TIMES WHEN I HAVE FORGOTTEN ABOUT YOUR GOODNESS. THERE HAVE BEEN TIMES WHEN I HAVE ALLOWED MYSELF TO ACCEPT YOUR LOVE BECAUSE IT IS CONSTANT BUT LOST MY APPRECIATION OF IT BECAUSE OF ITS CONSISTENCY. FORGIVE ME, LORD, AND REMIND ME TO REMEMBER THE CONSTANT NATURE OF YOUR LOVE. AMEN.

THE PEACE OF WORKING WELL

For we are his workmanship, created in Christ Jesus for good works, which God prepared ahead of time for us to do.

EPHESIANS 2:10

As I mentioned in the last entry, there is a peace that comes from acknowledging good work when you see it. There is an even greater peace that comes from a job well done. Whether you work in front of a screen, on the floor of a factory, or in the fields of a farm, a job well done comes with its moment of gratification and joy over the job being accomplished well.

We should always appreciate the work of others when we get the chance, and it is always nice when someone recognizes that we have done good work. But sometimes there are moments when we do not need recognition. Sometimes, we know full well that the work we have done is worthy of appreciation.

Few people exemplified this moment better than John and his brother, William. The two of them one summer were tasked with the job of building a fence around a field that would soon be filled with cattle. Post and barbed wire were given to them, and their only guidance was "just get it done." It was thirty acres of land that the boys had to fence. And they only had two months to do it. The good news was that this was their only task for the duration of the two months. They would not be required to complete the other chores on the farm as they would be too busy. The boys would arrive at the field ready to start fencing at six in the morning and leave at five in the evening. They would put in eleven-hour shifts every day. And every day, around noon, the boys would sit on the back of the truck, eat their lunch, and look at the distance they had covered. Each day, the length of the fence grew.

By the end of the first month, the boys had grown tedious of the work they were doing. They began to miss the chores and even consulted with their father about switching it up. The father told them that he had plans for them that would involve that field, so they needed to finish the fence. The boys continued, and with one week left, they slammed the final post into the ground and wrapped it with barbed wire.

As the two boys looked out at the field, they were proud. They did not need a clap on the back from their father because they knew the work that had been done by their hands. Years later, the two boys would stand before that field again as managers of the farm watching cattle that would have wandered if not for the good work done by the two of them.

LORD, THANK YOU FOR THE MOMENTS WHEN I HAVE BEEN ABLE TO DO GOOD WORK. ALLOW ME TO KEEP MY FOCUS ON THE WORK YOU HAVE SET BEFORE ME AND ALLOW ME TO DO IT WELL. AMEN.

CELEBRATING
THE GOOD

**The diligent hand will rule, but laziness
will lead to forced labor.**

PROVERBS 12:24

Celebration has its place in a devotional about stillness and peace. However, to celebrate the good, we need to acknowledge the cessation of the bad. At work, you may have spent countless hours putting together a project that you have finished. The late nights and early mornings can take a break, and you can now celebrate the goodness of the coming stillness. With family, there may have been a separation. You may have had to spend months and months apart from each other, and now that time of separation is over. It may even be something as simple as taking care of the chores of the home, and the celebration of the good may be something as simple as finally being able to relax.

Celebrating good work does not have to look like a party. It does not have to be loud. For some of us, the perfect celebration is collapsing into a couch and releasing a sigh of relief. We may have lost sleep, and the celebration might be catching up on those hours. You may be sore from a long day's work, taking a longer shower might be what you are after. Or maybe you have spent the day sitting and staring at a screen. Go outside by yourself and go for a walk.

However you decide to celebrate is up to you, but there is something to be said about enjoying the stillness after a long day's work. But what is the purpose of this celebration?

We do not rest because we just enjoy taking naps. That would point to laziness. We do not walk away to escape from our obligations. That would point to irresponsibility. No, the reason for good rest is the quiet celebration of good work. A spouse will let the other spouse rest in their favorite chair when they come home from work or after spending the day with the kids. These are pleasant moments, but the most important part of these moments is that they only come to those who earn them.

It does not matter how you celebrate, but it does matter how you have earned that celebration. If you have not done the work worth celebrating with rest, then you have not worked enough to earn rest. Do we sometimes need to rest in the moments when work is overwhelming? Yes! Of course! But the celebration of rest can only come to those who know they have finished a great task.

LORD, I AM TIRED. I KNOW I NEED TO REST. LORD, I THANK YOU FOR THE HARD WORK I HAVE DONE TODAY. I CAN REST KNOWING I HAVE EARNED IT. ALLOW ME TO KNOW THAT I NEED TO PUT IN WORK TO ENJOY AND CELEBRATE THE REST THAT COMES FROM IT. PUT IN ME A HEART THAT DESIRES TO WORK HARD SO I MAY ENJOY THE REST THAT COMES FROM HARD WORK. AMEN.

WHEN GOALS
ARE MET

**May he give you what your heart desires
and fulfill your whole purpose.**

PSALM 20:4

If you have been a part of any workplace in the past ten years, you may have come to realize the importance of goal setting in the workplace. At every performance review, the prospect of goal setting takes up at least a fourth of the conversation. Goals, however, when met, can provide a longing desire to make the dreams a little bigger the next time, but even more so provides a feeling of peace in knowing competence.

For Barbara, she openly hates the process. She says that the only goal she cares about is doing her job well. As a church secretary, she is not sure what kind of plans she should even be making. In one staff meeting, she jokingly asked, "What do you want me to do? Type faster?" She loves her church. She has been there the longest out of any of the current staff. She has clearly shown that she is invested in the church. Should not her goals be centered around that continued investment? One afternoon, while preparing for the staff meeting, she showed frustration about her goals in front of the student pastor.

The student pastor was an achiever. He loved goals, and Barbara thought that attitude was nauseating. Nevertheless, she asked about how to shape her goals. The student pastor challenged Barbara to pick something she cares

161

about first. He asked her to come up with one thing she had always admired but never done. After a moment of thinking, she said that she wanted to give financial control to her husband. The student pastor asked when she wanted to accomplish that. When she provided no precise deadline, he asked her why there was no deadline. While answering the question, she inadvertently admitted that she did not want to find disappointment if it did not happen.

In that, she realized the problem. She did want to set a goal that had a chance of failing. It was at this moment the student pastor said that it was rarely about accomplishing the goals. It was more about shooting for them, but he did admit that there was a tremendous peace from meeting a goal. He even said that once you do it, you can catch a bug that will make you want to set bigger ones. Barbara did not know about all that, but she agreed to set a date for her husband to take control of the finances. She chose April 15th on the calendar. In May, her husband was filling out budget spreadsheets.

HEAVENLY FATHER, I KNOW THERE ARE MOMENTS WHEN I HAVE BEEN AFRAID TO ACT BOLDLY ON WHAT YOU HAVE CALLED ME TO DO. PLEASE ALLOW ME TO MOVE FORWARD IN WHAT YOU DESIRE FOR ME. THANK YOU FOR THE PEACE THAT COMES FROM FOLLOWING YOUR WILL AND GIVE ME THE WILL TO DO IT WELL. AMEN.

THE PEACE OF TRUSTWORTHINESS

"These are the things you must do: Speak truth to
one another; make true and sound decisions within
your city gates. Do not plot evil in your hearts
against your neighbor, and do not love perjury, for
I hate all this"—this is the Lord's declaration.

ZECHARIAH 8:16–17

A trustworthy person can bring peace to the room no matter the personality attached to that person. If they are kind, we can know that they care about our feelings while giving us hard news. If blunt, we can rest in knowing that the information is not going to be sugarcoated. Peace does not necessarily have to be sweet. We have misunderstood this in our culture. We have assumed that to be a caring person, others should find us synonymous with rainbows and gumdrops. Politeness does not always equal niceness. After all, how many of us have wished our spouses were honest with us about what we were wearing?

There is something to be said about a person you can trust. If we took a moment, we could think of the person in our life who we trust the most. For this one, I am not necessarily speaking about the ones we go to in confidence. Trusting a person with a secret is good, but I am speaking of the people who will tell you what is on their minds. They will not hide it from you, and they will not skirt around their thoughts if you ask for their opinion. Their delivery may be different, but the truth remains the same.

Do you have that person in your head right now? Think about their character. Think about your friendship with them. If we are honest with ourselves, we both love and hate this characteristic about them. We never know if what they say is going to be what we want to hear. That does not change the fact that we still need to listen. And even though there are moments when we will not enjoy their words, there is a peace in them. We know that we can trust them.

We understand that even though they may not give us the news or thoughts that we want, we know that it is what they believe, nothing more or less. Do not undervalue the peace that comes from a trustworthy friend. If you still have that person in your mind, you are thinking of every frustrating conversation you have had with them, only to end the discussion with a yielding, "I know you're right." This person, whether you like it or not, is probably your best friend, and if you do not think they are, you know they should be.

Thank God for friends who tell us like it is, those who do not pull any punches. We have the opportunity sometimes to soften their delivery, but we would never do anything to stop valuing the truth being told. There is too much peace in that.

LORD, THANK YOU FOR HONESTY AND THANK YOU FOR MY MOST HONEST FRIENDS. REMIND ME TO SHOW APPRECIATION FOR THESE PEOPLE AND ALLOW ME TO GLEAN FROM THEM AND SHARE THE SAME KIND OF HONESTY WITH OTHERS. AMEN.

THE WORST THEY CAN SAY IS "NO"

**Yet you do not know what tomorrow will bring—
what your life will be! For you are like vapor
that appears for a little while, then vanishes.**

JAMES 4:14

This piece of wisdom has been heard by just about every thirteen-year-old boy at least once. They find a girl who they like. They want to ask her to the school dance but are not sure if the risk of rejection is worth asking the question in the first place. And yet, every nugget of wisdom often tells these young men to take the chance and put themselves out there to have their offer rejected or accepted. Even though rejection may hurt, there is no peace greater than knowing the answer in its finality.

A young boy named Riley would learn this lesson well. The winter dance was quickly approaching, and he had his sights set on Kimberly Fisher. She was one of the girls who lived at Olympus-level heights in the eyes of Riley. He was a mortal. She was a goddess, and that is all there was to it. He did not assume he had a chance with her. He was president of the art club and kept to a small circle of friends. He played soccer, but other than that, he was not known for his athleticism. For him, the best he could offer was at the annual art show. That is where his talents shined. Luckily for him, the art show was in the first week of November, and it was customary to start asking girls to the dance in the second week.

She came to the art show, as all students did, and remarked at how talented he was and even asked if he would consider painting a picture of her family's dog that she could give to her parents for Christmas. She offered to pay him, but he said that it would not be necessary. For Riley, he would take all the help he could get.

That whole week, the two got to know each other. They laughed as Kimberly helped keep the dog still while Riley sketched out shapes that would help him paint later. By the end of the week, the two had become closer, and slowly, Kimberly left Olympus and started to look more and more human. Somehow, this made Riley more nervous. At least if she said no a week ago, it would have been because he felt that they had nothing in common.

After a week, the two had a few moments of innocent flirtation as infatuated teens always do, and when he delivered the final painting to her house she was overjoyed. She hugged him and said that she loved it. When she let him go, Riley gulped and asked. After all, the worst she could say is "No," right?

HEAVENLY FATHER, I KNOW THERE ARE TIMES WHEN IT TAKES THE COURAGE TO ACT. I KNOW I HAVE BEEN GUILTY OF NOT ACTING WHEN I SHOULD BECAUSE OF FEAR OF THE OUTCOME. REMIND ME OF THE PEACE THAT COMES FROM KNOWING WHAT SHOULD BE DONE AND THE PEACE THAT COMES FROM HAVING DONE THAT WHICH YOU HAVE CALLED ME TO DO. AMEN.

THE ANXIETY OF
THE JOB INTERVIEW

Jesus spoke to them again: "I am the light of the
world. Anyone who follows me will never walk
in the darkness but will have the light of life."

JOHN 8:12

There is a split between two kinds of people when looking for a job. Some enjoy the process, and others loathe it. For those who find it fun, they like the prospect of highlighting their best qualities. They enjoy showing how they will be an asset to the work. On the other hand, some do their best to minimize their weaknesses so that the potential employer will see past their flaws and hire them anyway. One thing that does not seem to matter, however, is the last hours before a job interview. There is an apprehension that seems to overcome the emotions of applicants. Even if only for a moment, nervousness robs them of their confidence.

If you have ever had a job, you know the moment I am describing. You more than likely sat in the parking lot for anywhere between five and thirty minutes. You prepared for the most challenging questions. You looked at your reflection in the mirror to make sure that you were presentable. You fixed your clothes one last time, confirming that nothing was untucked, unbuttoned, or unzipped. And for one last time, you show all thirty-two of your teeth in the mirror to ensure that nothing is sitting in the gaps between them.

Then, you get out of the car and start walking toward the building. Whether greeted by a receptionist, an assistant, or the boss, you smile, offer a firm, but not too firm, handshake, and walk into a room for interviews. Every second of this interview is a mix of emotions that try to make you look relaxed, but not too casual that you appear to be informal. You sit up straight, but not so straight that you come off as a stick in the mud. Your prerogative is balance. You want to be confident but not cocky. You are looking for the sweet spot between fun to work with and professional. It is a challenging tightrope to walk. And yet, many of us forget something incredibly important.

We are not the first to sit in that chair. The person interviewing us more than likely sat in that chair as well. They had the same emotions you felt. Even though they may have a different role, they also had to start somewhere, being asked questions that are difficult to answer.

When we know we are not the first person to go through what we are going through, we experience a bit of relief. We can let go of some of the tension. Know that you are not alone. Others have stood where you are. If they made it, so can you.

LORD, ALLOW ME TO REST IN KNOWING THAT THE PATH YOU HAVE SET BEFORE ME IS NOT ONE THAT OTHERS HAVE NOT ALSO WALKED. REMIND ME THAT YOUR SON PROVIDED A PATH TO FOLLOW AND I AM NOT THE ONLY ONE WALKING IT. AMEN.

THE FIRST NIGHT
SHE SLEPT

**Listen, my son, to your father's instruction,
and don't reject your mother's teaching.**

PROVERBS 1:8

As new parents, Lyla and Michael had prepared for parenthood as much as anyone could. They read the right books, listened to the right podcasts, and consulted the best doctors. They dedicated themselves to protecting the health of their newborn daughter. So, when she was born, it was understandable that they had approached the situation with cautious optimism. They felt prepared. When their baby girl came home, however, they started realizing that all the books in the world could not prepare them for the late nights that would be spent feeding, rocking, and lulling her to sleep.

They, however, were dedicated to the plan. And in four months, their little girl slept through her first night all on her own. For Lyla and Michael, no book, podcast, or doctor could fully explain the peace that comes from the first night of uninterrupted sleep. At seven in the evening, Lyla laid down her little girl in her crib. She turned on soft music and crept away for the evening. For the first hour, however, she watched the baby monitor and felt a sense of sadness. Her little girl, in four months, had made it to where she no longer needed the rocking motion of her parents to fall asleep. It was surreal. For weeks, she had looked forward to the day when she would make it through a night of uninterrupted sleep. And yet, now Lyla was watching her baby sleep and longed for the baby to need her mother to fall back asleep.

Michael saw the sadness on his wife's face—knowing she was missing her daughter. He leaned over and kissed her on the head and said, "She may not need you to sleep through the night anymore, but she will need you for countless things in the future."

Lyla knew this was true and wiped away the solitary tear building in the corner of her eye. Then, she picked up the phone to call her mom and ask if she was crazy for feeling this way. While on the phone with her mother, catching up and talking about early motherhood, Lyla realized the truth of her husband's words. Here she was in her late twenties, asking her mother for help. Lyla no longer needed her mom to fall asleep, but she still consulted her for wisdom. She never lost that and treasured every moment she could have with her mom in this new stage of life.

Sometimes we forget the gift that parents are. We forget the importance of having them in our lives. There are countless things that we no longer need parents for, but if you have been lucky enough to keep them in your life, you have realized that what you have them for now is just as important.

HEAVENLY FATHER, THANK YOU FOR THE WISDOM FROM FAMILY. THANK YOU FOR GIVING ME PEOPLE WHO I CAN RELY ON FOR HELP IN TIMES WHEN I DO NOT KNOW WHAT TO DO. AMEN.

SETTING A RHYTHM

Pay careful attention, then, to how you walk—not as unwise people but as wise—making the most of the time, because the days are evil. So don't be foolish, but understand what the Lord's will is.

EPHESIANS 5:15–17

In all things, there is nothing quite like a set rhythm. Even though we should not marry ourselves to a routine, there is nothing wrong with having an established schedule to live by. For instance, you may find a run at six in the morning is just the thing you need to keep your spirits up throughout the day. An early afternoon snack may carry your hunger to dinner. And no one could disagree that there is anything wrong with scheduling uninterrupted time slots for work. Even though flexibility is something to be appreciated and expected, a good and well-kept schedule can provide ample amounts of peace in the long run.

No one exemplifies this better than Emily. She is a woman who lives by her schedule. She has a digital planner that captures daily tasks like exercise, meals, phone calls, and reminders of upcoming events. She owns a faux leather planner that catalogs every notable date for the year. She spends the afternoon of New Year's Eve filling it out. Then, throughout the year, she fills in other dates as they come. If all of that was not enough, hung on her wall at home is a whiteboard calendar that she uses to fill in responsibilities. If it is for the church, she writes in blue. If it is for work, she writes in green. If it is family-related, she writes in orange, and if it personal, she writes in red.

There is very little about her life that is not planned. Now, before you say that she is a little too dedicated to living by a schedule, she is very quick to defend herself that everything that is written can be erased. Her planner is in pencil, her phone has the option to delete, and the whiteboard uses dry-erase markers. She likes a schedule, but she knows that not everything can go according to plan. And to be fair, we cannot argue with the peace she carries with her throughout the week. She understands that she needs structure, and there is nothing wrong with that. Many would even argue that this is an exemplary form of proper stewardship of one's time.

Things are not going to go to plan. Ask any minister and the majority of them will have a story where they thought that they would be doing something else. The kinds of plans being discussed here are not wrong. It is completely acceptable and even encouraged to know what you need to take care of yourself. For Emily, that just means giving a bit of structure, and as long as she is not making that the source of her peace, then we could all take this as a lesson to improve our time management.

HEAVENLY FATHER, THANK YOU FOR GIVING ME THE ABILITY TO KNOW MYSELF. ALLOW ME TO APPROACH MY NEEDS WITH HONESTY AND TAKE CARE OF MY NEEDS IN A WAY THAT BRINGS GLORY TO YOU. AMEN.

85

MAKING A PLAN

And be kind and compassionate to one another, forgiving one another, just as God also forgave you in Christ.

EPHESIANS 4:32

Hayden and his wife love to go on vacation. They live minimally in just about every area, but their extravagance is shown on their yearly trip. They have traveled around the world and found ways to save money here and there to make the most out of their time away. Hayden will put together a plan that captures price and timing to have a basic understanding of their destination before they even board their first flight. His wife, Nikki, loves discovering restaurants that are not mentioned in travel blogs and witnessing views that are off the beaten path. Nikki makes the plans for the vacation itinerary, and Hayden makes sure that they do everything on the list in a time-efficient and budget-friendly way.

By doing this, they find a tremendous level of peace before they ever leave the driveway. The most important lesson they have learned from this, however, is that if something does not go according to plan, it is going to be okay. The fun is not in the trip itself. It is in traveling with each other. There have been times when a flight has been delayed. A layover lasted longer than expected. There was a miscommunication about the rental car. Their room was not ready at the time of check-in. They have learned that a road is not a road unless there are bumps in it.

When they were younger, these kinds of occurrences would infuriate them. They would demand refunds, ask to speak to managers, and expect upgrades for their treatment. Not only did these attitudes not yield fruit, but they also ended up angry at something fixable. Their attitudes, however, shifted when they shared the same frustration as an elderly couple who happened to be traveling to the same destination.

All four of them were going to northern California. Hayden and Nikki were going to see the redwoods. The couple was traveling to visit their grandchildren. Somehow, there had been a mix-up with the luggage, and now all parties going to California would hear that their luggage was heading to North Carolina. The airline had already heard about this issue and had the luggage swapped during the flight's layover in Dallas. The luggage would get to the airport in six hours. Hayden was furious. That would mean that they were going to miss their check-in time for their cabin rental and would have to pay for a night at the hotel next door. He marched up to the desk to have a word with the woman sitting behind it. The old man, however, had beat him to the counter, and Hayden overheard the conversation.

"Ma'am, how long have you been here?" the old man said.

With tired eyes, she looked up at him and said, "I'm covering a shift, I've been here 11 hours."

"Goodness!" he exclaimed. "Have you had anything to eat?"

Hayden was shocked at the question but watched as the woman softened and assisted the man and even provided him with a free meal voucher for them to have a meal. He was disappointed in himself. Hayden was ready to go to someone who had done nothing wrong and treat them with contempt. That moment shifted the way he traveled, and if he were honest about that moment's impact, he would say it changed the way he lived.

FATHER, REMIND ME TO TREAT OTHERS
WITH KINDNESS WHEN THINGS DO
NOT GO MY WAY. AMEN.

174

86

THE CHAIR EXERCISE

Therefore, he is able to save completely those who come to God through him, since he always lives to intercede for them.

HEBREWS 7:25

When the teenagers of a church came for the Wednesday night youth group, they were surprised to find all of the chairs that were usually in a circle were now in a straight line. When they sat down together, each of them shoulder to shoulder, the youth pastor asked them to play a couple games of telephone. They whispered little messages from one person to the next, each of them laughing at the ridiculous sentences that ended each round. After their third round, the pastor asked one student to start a message, but this time the game would only be played with two. After each round, however, the student would move down a seat and try to get the information from the messenger. By the end of the fifth round, the student could not make out any of the messages that were being sent.

Some students would try their hand at seeing if they could beat the five-seat record. Some came close, but unless you could make out what the original message was perfectly it did not count. When the fun of the game started to wane, the youth pastor asked his students if they knew the game's purpose. One student raised his hand and said, "We have to listen to each other?"

The youth pastor tilted his head in somewhat agreement. He said, "That is important, but it is not the message of the activity. It is close, though! Anyone else?"

Another student raised his hand. "The further we are from other people, the less we can hear from them?"

The youth pastor grinned and straightened up and said, "You are so close! Let's try something else."

The youth pastor had a seat and opened his Bible. He asked for one of the students to volunteer for a different form of the game. One of his senior boys came and sat down next to him. He asked him to repeat after him. In the first verse, he did well. He did not make any mistakes. He asked him to move down a seat, but pretend he cheated on his math test. He moved down a seat, holding that thought in his head. The youth pastor read another verse, and the student repeated him. When he moved down this time, the youth pastor asked him to pretend that he had been confronted by his teacher about the test and that he lied.

This time, he moved down again, holding onto two sins. Admittedly, he had a little trouble saying the next verse. With each move, the youth pastor added another sin, and the student moved until he could no longer recite the verse. At the end of the exercise, the youth pastor gave the lesson: the further you move from God, the harder it is to hear Him.

HEAVENLY FATHER, I KNOW I HAVE WANDERED FROM YOU. I KNOW THERE IS SIN THAT I HAVE LEFT UNRESOLVED. PLEASE ALLOW ME TO FIND REST IN YOU AGAIN AND COME BEFORE YOU AND SEEK FORGIVENESS. AMEN.

NOISE-CANCELING EARBUDS

Immediately he made the disciples get into the boat and go ahead of him to the other side, while he dismissed the crowds. After dismissing the crowds, he went up on the mountain by himself to pray. Well into the night, he was there alone.

MATTHEW 14:22–23

Noise-canceling earbuds are all the rage right now. They are expensive because the technology is both new and available, but everyone wants a pair. Their greatest benefit being discussed is the truly wireless nature of the devices. Listeners no longer have to worry about a wire getting caught and pulling their earbud from their ear, but for the listeners, the best available feature of the technology is its ability to block out surrounding noise.

Headphones have been around for decades, but only recently have they had the kind of technology to block out surrounding sound. We all know what I am describing. You are sitting on a bus or mowing the lawn, and you want to hear what is coming out of the headphones: nothing else. Headphones finally started providing this technology at an affordable rate, but they are clunky and difficult to store. This is when earbuds came into the picture. They provided music that a listener could securely place in their ear. By their design alone, they offered a way to block out some of the distractions. They allowed the listener to go to their quiet place anywhere. Then, a few years later, they added the technology to actively silence the distractions of the world.

What is incredible about these, however, is not found in their technology. What is extraordinary about these devices is what it says about our society. One of the valuable pieces of available technology is found in its ability to block out the noise. The marketability of these devices communicates the reality that this world is loud, and people all over the world are seeking silence. They are seeking peace. They have a desire to block out the world.

As Christians, we should not be surprised by this. We should not be surprised by the reality that people, in the end, do not want the noise of the world. It can be enticing at first. But when it comes down to what people truly desire, the commodity is quiet.

We live in a noisy world. With every distraction, it is obvious that this life is one that can be consumed with chaos if we are not careful. But we have a refuge. We have a quiet place, and we serve a God who provides peace beyond all understanding.

LORD, I COME TO YOU THIS DAY TO BLOCK OUT THE NOISE. I WANT MY FOCUS TO BE COMPLETELY ON YOU. I WANT TO EXPERIENCE THE QUIET PEACE, THE TRUST, AND THE JOY THAT COMES FROM KNOWING YOU. ALLOW ME TO LEAVE THE NOISE BEHIND AND COME TO YOU. ALLOW ME TO FIND THE QUIET AND SPEND MY TIME IN SILENCE READING YOUR WORD AND KNOWING YOU MORE. AMEN.

UNENDING
CONVERSATION

**A wise correction to a receptive ear is like
a gold ring or an ornament of gold.**
PROVERBS 25:12

Clear communication is probably the most valuable asset to a healthy marriage. Many, if not all of us, would agree with this. There is, however, something to be said about the listening side of communication. Beverly jokes that her husband is not a good communicator even though he is a professor in the communications department. Her husband's greatest problem is not that he does not communicate. Instead, his issue is that he overcommunicates. The majority of their conversations are one-sided. Beverly listens, and her husband goes on and on about the happenings of his day. Communication cannot come from only one source.

Her husband learned this when he agreed to take up ownership over the debate team of the school. His first strategy as a coach would be to give so much information on why their side was correct that no argument could be made. If you have witnessed a debate or participated in one, you can understand how flawed this logic is. In their first debate, they took a stance on an economic issue that was occurring in the world. The professor's team used every ounce of their time to explain why their thoughts on the topic were the correct ones. The reason this was such a flaw was shown when the opposing side never mentioned one of the argument points. They spent their time taking apart their opponents' arguments. Flustered, Beverly's husband approached her after the debate, and said, "I did not expect to win, but I did not expect to lose so embarrassingly."

While comforting her husband, Beverly asked, "Can you recall anything the other team said?"

Beverly watched the thought dawn on her husband. He realized that she was right about the debate. But then his face shifted from thoughtful to guilty. He had realized that she was not only talking about the debate stage. He asked, "What should I do?"

For a moment, Beverly was taken aback. It was rare for her husband to ask her to speak. He was not abusive or rude. He just had a lot of words. She kissed him on the cheek, rested her head on his shoulder, and softly said, "There is just as much worth to those who listen for the right words as those who speak them."

At the next debate, the team still lost, but this time, under the professor's direction, they at least put up a decent fight. When everything was finished, Beverly's husband approached her, sat next to her, and asked, "How do you think it went?" Then, he was quiet and waited to listen to his wife's words.

DEAR LORD, I KNOW I HAVE NOT LISTENED FOR YOUR GUIDANCE IN THE WAY THAT I SHOULD. THERE ARE MOMENTS WHEN I ENTER PRAYER READY TO SPEAK BUT AM RARELY READY TO LISTEN. STILL ME, LORD. GIVE ME THE PATIENCE TO HEAR WHAT YOU WANT TO SAY TO ME. AMEN.

ONE MISSED EMAIL

**Then they brought the boats to land,
left everything, and followed him.**

LUKE 5:11

George does not know how to take a vacation. Frankly, he has not taken one since he took his last job. George is the kind of employee who works into the night. He goes the extra mile on different projects and will answer any email regardless of the time. There are even a couple of emails with timestamps well outside of working hours. It makes sense that he panics whenever he misses an email.

This dedication to work had never been a problem for the family. After all, he worked hard so that his family did not have to. He put in long hours so that his wife could stay home with the kids. What is so wrong with that? Well, it became a problem when his phone died while he was on vacation with his family. His wife had reluctantly agreed to allow him to answer emails while they were on the trip, but he could not look at his phone during meals. It seemed easy enough to follow. He kept his phone on silent during meals and flipped over so he could not see any notifications pop up during the dinner.

When he stood up to use the restroom, however, a waitress tripped and spilled water all over his phone, making it utterly useless. George's wife watched panic wash over his face and told him to go take a walk before he said something he regretted. He was angry. He was terrified. How would his employees be able to reach him if he did not have his phone? He started trying to figure out how he could get to a phone store and find a replacement as soon as possible.

After a couple of minutes of pacing, George's wife came and found her husband in the parking lot. She said, "I think you might just care about your work more than you care about me and the kids."

Not wanting to admit it, he said, "I know you're right. I just need to work."

With patience, she challenged him, "If you have more than one missed email, and that leads you to lose your job, I will get a job and never bother you about the phone again."

He agreed. The week passed, and he had no phone. And as much as he would hate to admit it, he had fun with his kids and his wife. There was freedom by letting go of work's responsibilities. When he finally returned to work, he expected a slew of emails. He assumed he would have four or five from his boss demanding to know where he was. He only had one email. It was from his boss, and it said, "Your wife called and said for no one to bother you while you were on vacation. Do not check your email this week."

LORD, I KNOW I HAVE PUT SO MANY THINGS IN FRONT OF THAT WHICH MATTERS THE MOST. FORGIVE ME FOR THAT AND REMIND ME TO KEEP FIRST WHAT SHOULD BE FIRST. AMEN.

ARE YOU CONNECTED?

Do not have other gods besides me.

EXODUS 20:3

There is no panic quite like the one that covers the minds of those who lose Internet connection. It always seems to happen at the worst times. Our connection cuts out when we were just about to send an important email. The Internet stops working when we are halfway through a movie. The streaming service freezes during the cliffhanger of the season finale of whatever show we are viewing. Even if you have never felt any of these, you have more than likely felt the discomfort that comes from losing access to the Internet.

In one way, it is sad because it is just another example that shows how we have become a little too reliant on technology. But in another sense, it paints a good picture of the importance of being connected to that which is most important. When some of us lose our access to the Internet, we lose entertainment, our ability to work, and our ability to check in with family and loved ones. But what happens when we lose our connection to God?

The sad reality is that many of us have lost that feeling of connection with the Lord and have shown little frustration. Maybe you left your Bible at home when you went to church. Maybe you forgot to grab a pen to take notes during the sermon. Think about the time the fellowship event was canceled. Were you as frustrated in those moments as you were when you lost Wi-Fi?

Think about the moment you returned to your phone after a nap or a busy day. How long did it take you to check any notifications for social media? The purpose of today's entry was not to make you feel guilty for having a desire to stay connected to the Internet. Wi-Fi is not sinful, but if we have more excitement over getting back online than spending time with the Lord after a long day, then we may have an idol on our hands.

The Internet has changed the very nature of the way we live in this world. Half of the American companies offer some form of work that can be done remotely. One in three people finds love on a dating site. The majority of homes have a video game console that allows people to play with others all over the world. High school classes are even being offered that discuss the nuance involved in online communication.

Face it. We almost have to use the Internet. This is not a bad thing. And if we are honest, we have a love for it because it provides an avenue for connection. But the connection to the Internet is faulty. It is man-made after all. It lacks perfection. The kind of connection that we should be after is our connection to God. It never fails. We always have access to Him.

DEAR GOD, I KNOW I HAVE MISSED OUT ON MOMENTS TO CONNECT WITH YOU. I WANT TO NOT CARE SO MUCH ABOUT THE CONNECTION THAT THIS WORLD OFFERS AND SEEK TO BE MORE CONNECTED TO YOU. AMEN.

DRIVE-THRU PATIENCE

I wait for the LORD; I wait and
put my hope in his word.

PSALM 130:5

Many understand that patience is a virtue, but what makes it valuable to the person who possesses extraordinary patience? Why is peace provided to the one who knows how to wait? The reality is that many of us miss out on the joy of being patient. There is an addition to the life of a person who can be surrounded by time's obscurity and have faith that there will be an end to the waiting.

In our current circumstances, the drive-thru has become a staple to the American way of living. The days of waiting in line for a meal, taking one's tray, and having a seat are over. People no longer have to stand in line. Even though restaurants still do their best to streamline the dine-in experience, there is nothing quite like the ability to pull up to a window, grab one's food, and take it home to eat. Some meals, however, only make it to a parking spot.

So, it is of no surprise that we have shifted from the introduction of good service to expecting it when we arrive at a restaurant. Now, we feel inconvenienced if the drive-thru process takes longer than five minutes. While we wait in our air-conditioned vehicles, listening to what we want, ordering what we want, and inching forward to receive what we want, we assume that we have been inconvenienced if we do not receive it right when we want it. Even worse, some of us have probably patted ourselves on the back for being so gracious when the window asks us to pull forward to wait just a little longer for our food.

It all sounds a little ludicrous to think about the drive-thru process and throw the virtue of patience in there. But even there, the opportunities to exercise patience are key. Besides, all patience is an exercise in trust and humility. We trust that we placed our order clearly. We humbly wait in line behind five or six cars, assuming that the line will shorten little by little. We thank the people who take our money and appreciate the people who hand us our food. All of these fall under the umbrella of patience.

The value of patience is not found in our ability to wait. That is only part of it. The value of patience is discovered in how we wait. We wait in the trust of the one we are waiting for. We rest in humility by trusting that whatever is said to be on its way will come the way it said. It's kind of like waiting in the drive-thru gives a little window in how we should wait for the Lord. Trust that what He has planned for you is coming. Know that His call on your life will happen, and be willing to wait for however long it will take. It may take longer than your time in the drive-thru, but I would challenge you to adopt the attitude of one who can patiently wait for that which is promised to come.

LORD, I KNOW THERE HAVE BEEN TIMES WHEN MY PATIENCE HAS BEEN TESTED, AND I HAVE FAILED THAT TEST. PLEASE ALLOW ME TO BE ABLE TO WAIT ON THAT WHICH YOU WOULD HAVE FOR ME WITH TRUST AND HUMILITY. AMEN.

92

DAD'S HAMMOCK

Just as each one has received a gift, use it to serve others, as good stewards of the varied grace of God.

1 PETER 4:10

In the backyard of Collin's house is a hammock reserved for his father. During the Indiana summers, Collin's father will collapse into the hammock and spend the better part of an hour or so reading. Now, Collin is an adventurous child. He sees his father's hammock more like a swing than a glorified couch. When it is open, Collin will lie in it and rock back and forth, building the momentum to the point where there is a bit of danger in its swaying. However, when his father approaches the hammock with a book in hand, Collin hops out of the hammock and runs off to entertain himself with something else. He understands that the purpose of the hammock has morphed from entertainment to rest.

As Collin grew older, he learned to appreciate the hammock through the lens that his father had. It hung between two perfectly distanced trees. The side where his father's head rested was a little more elevated to provide a view of the lake. And over time, a dip had formed where his father rested his head. This provided almost a perfect cradle for his father as he read his books. This hammock's placement had matched up with the purpose his father gave it.

In the Christian life, many of us can benefit from living out the purpose we have all been given. There is confidence when you know that you are doing what you have been called to do. The reality is that God has given us the ability to do incredible things. He has made some of us good speakers. He has given some of us sound minds. He has provided talent for the artistic ones and given sharpness to the intellectual ones. He has gifted some people with special ingenuity. These gifts are not to be taken lightly. After all, if you have been given something, you received it with a purpose in mind.

God gives tremendous gifts to every person with tremendous things in mind. Now, that may sound a little daunting. How does answering a call give peace? How does taking on an opportunity provide the chance for stillness? Well, when we do what we have been called to do, when we use the gifts that have so clearly been given, then we get to live knowing that we are doing what God has called us to do. To do the opposite of what God wants naturally brings anxiety, shame, and frustration. To take part in God's plan and using the gifts He has given provides opportunities for joy, celebration, and peace.

LORD, I THANK YOU FOR ALL OF THE GIFTS YOU HAVE GIVEN ME. I THANK YOU FOR THE CHANCE TO TAKE PART IN YOUR PLAN FOR MY LIFE. GIVE ME THE COURAGE TO STEP BOLDLY FOR YOU, AND PEACE IN KNOWING THAT I HAVE DONE IT WELL. AMEN.

93

THE FIVE-HOUR LAYOVER

*Everyone should look not to his own interests,
but rather to the interests of others.*

PHILIPPIANS 2:4

If you have ever been to an airport, you have probably dealt with a layover of some sort. Some travelers have dealt with the panic of a thirty-minute layover. They have sprinted from one terminal to the next to make their flight. Others have had the comfort of one that lasts a couple of hours. They casually stroll to their flight. Grab a snack and take a seat. Many travelers have said that even when they are in a hurry to get to their destination, they would rather have a two-hour layover than one that can cause them to almost miss their flight.

Sometimes, however, a person will have to endure a rather long layover. This happened to Patrick on his way home from a convention. During his journey to his home in Charleston from Los Angeles, he found himself in the Dallas airport waiting on his next flight. Because of a weather delay, however, his layover would last five hours instead of two hours.

Many airports provide special opportunities for frequent travelers. You get special meal vouchers, access to special privileges, and many more opportunities. Some travelers, however, would trade all of the amenities for the chance to get to their destination. Patrick was in the latter. He was ready to be home, and even though Patrick flew frequently, he did not travel often enough to enjoy all of the bells and whistles that come from being a frequent flyer. He did not have access to any of the fancy distractions. So, what did he do? He stood, gathered his things, and went for a walk. He had heard that Dallas had one of the largest airports in the world. So, he decided that he was going to find out just how large it was.

As he walked, he caught glimpses of joy. He saw couples breathe sighs of relief by having the chance to spend just a couple more hours with each other. He saw grandchildren nuzzle into the arms of their grandparents, knowing they would get to spend a few more moments with family.

Patrick realized that even though he was ready to go home, his waiting provided joy for others. If he had gotten his way for a few hours of convenience, many people would have missed out on being able to slow down and enjoy the moment just a little longer. Patrick found a purpose in his waiting. Just remember. God may call you to wait for the benefit of others. Patrick had to wait for a few more hours, but his delay provided joy to others. God sometimes gives us inconvenience to see the good it provides others.

LORD, I KNOW THERE ARE MOMENTS WHEN I HAVE BEEN IMPATIENT AND ASSUMED THAT MY TIME WAS ONLY ABOUT ME. PLEASE PROVIDE ME WITH MOMENTS TO KNOW THAT OTHERS MAY NEED THE EXTRA TIME AND THAT MY PATIENCE CAN IN MANY WAYS BE A GIFT TO THEM. AMEN.

THE TWO-WEEK TRAIN RIDE

*When I observe your heavens, the
work of your fingers, the moon and the
stars, which you set in place.*

PSALM 8:3

There is a train ride that has become famous in the past few years. It takes two weeks, starts in Chicago, and ends in northern California. Though the ride might be extensive, the train offers a "sky car" made primarily out of plexiglass that allows the viewer to witness the majestic scenery that the American landscape has to offer. And even though it may not be the most comfortable ride, a person can travel this route for as little as $98. Now, to be fair, that is two weeks in a seated position with access only to public showers. I suggest getting a room in one of the cars. It may be a bit more expensive, but you have the luxury of a bed and a private bathroom.

When Marie approached her husband about the opportunity, he dismissed her desire for a unique travel experience. After a couple of months of begging, however, he finally relented and agreed to do some research on the trip. He had discovered that his boss would allow him to work from the train as long as he had Internet access. With that being his largest objection to going on the trip, they had their tickets in a few weeks. The two of them were in their mid-twenties. They had enough money to travel frugally but could not leave the country. So, Marie decided she would make the most out of her journey. They would stop at different places and explore whatever local attractions they could find. Marie was determined to cram five vacations in one.

Her husband was nervous. He had never traveled by train, and he questioned his wife's confidence. Nevertheless, they ordered the tickets and prepared to go from their home in Chicago to Los Angeles. When they first got to their seats, Marie was pleased to find a table with a charger so that her husband could work during the long drags of travel. He, admittedly, was comforted by the sight as well.

After their first four hours, Marie and her husband decided to stretch their legs. They walked to the dining car and received a meal. While walking back to their seats, they passed a sign that said, "Ask your conductor about access to the sky car! First-time riders get free access!" The two of them shrugged and took the sign up on its offer. When they asked the conductor to guide them, however, he refused. He said, "When it is this late in the day, you won't see anything. Try tomorrow morning."

When morning came, the conductor came to find them and guided them to the car. Amazement is a weak description of how the couple felt when standing in the plexiglass car. They saw the sunrise peak over the mountainous landscape of Colorado. With gaped mouths, they heard the conductor say, "When you rush by landscape in a plane or only have your eyes on the road, you miss out on why they call it God's artwork." He then left the two as they sat and sipped coffee, watching views rarely seen by those who are in too much of a rush to see them.

LORD, REMIND ME TO SLOW DOWN. ALLOW ME TO KNOW THAT IT IS IN THE MOMENTS WHEN I AM STILL THAT YOU SHOW ME THE MOST WONDROUS PARTS OF YOUR CREATION. AMEN.

95

QUIET DRIVES

"No one can serve two masters, since either
he will hate one and love the other, or he will
be devoted to one and despise the other."

MATTHEW 6:24

We are surrounded by stimulation. Whether you are watching a television screen, working through a computer screen, or seeking entertainment through your smartphone, the chances are that there is a lack of quiet in your life. It is because of this that we have learned the quickest way to find peace is probably going to be found by "unplugging" and walking away from technology.

For Alvin, he learned the best way to do this is to go for long drives in his old truck. The radio is broken, and the windows still have to be rolled down manually, but it still runs. And for him, that's all he needs. Every Saturday morning, he wakes up before the sun rises and tinkers in his workshop, but after that, he gets in his old truck and goes for a drive with nothing but the hum of an old engine to fill the silence.

For many of us, this sounds like a nightmare. How can you drive without any music? How can you travel without some form of entertainment? What benefit is there to the quiet? Many of us have come to hate silence. We listen to music. If we do not have music, we have podcasts. If we do not have access to that, then we will listen to audiobooks. And if for some reason we do not have access to our phones, we at least have the radio. The vast majority of us will do whatever it takes to escape silence. And yet, Alvin seeks it. He longs to escape the noise.

What is the reason for this? Well, the reality is that he loves stimulation, and he loves the Lord. He knows that he cannot have both. So, on Saturdays, he leaves these behind. When he drives, there may be silence at first, but most of the time is spent with Alvin talking to God and listening for a word from Him. He prays every day. He makes sure to read his Bible as regularly as he can, but Alvin knows the special attention it takes to spend intentional time in prayer with the Lord. He removes distraction. He eliminates outside stimulation and spends time with the Lord in silence.

Even though it is difficult for us to admit, our time with the Lord is spent with distraction in the room. The things of this world pop in and interfere with quiet time with God. So, at the end of the day, we have to ask ourselves, who do we serve? God? Or the distractions that keep us from being with Him?

LORD, I KNOW THERE HAVE BEEN TIMES WHEN I HAVE SERVED TWO MASTERS. I ASK FOR YOUR FORGIVENESS IN THIS. PLEASE REMIND ME OF YOUR LOVE AND PEACE AND GIVE ME THE OPPORTUNITIES TO LEAVE THE DISTRACTIONS AND SPEND MORE TIME WITH YOU. AMEN.

96

I NEED TO THINK

Do you see someone who speaks too soon?
There is more hope for a fool than for him.

PROVERBS 29:20

Whenever Jordan says, "I need to think," his wife is well-aware of what comes next. He will go for a drive, grab a soda from the local gas station, and listen to the radio for about a half-hour. His wife has learned not to take it personally. It is just that when life provides a bit of stress, Jordan learned the importance of taking a moment to think before he makes a decision. He has learned to steady his mind.

So many of us are quick to jump at the chance to make a decision. We desperately want to have an answer right then and there for the different situations that pop in the day-to-day. And even though we desire to have immediate wisdom to handle questionable tasks with efficiency, we understand that this is not always going to be this way. Rarely do we ever know the right answer at the exact moment when we receive a question. The mark of the wise is not in the ability to answer questions quickly. It is in the ability to answer questions thoughtfully.

Thoughtfulness is one of the strongest indicators of wisdom. It does not only show the ability to provide an answer to frustration. But instead, it shows that you care enough about the issue to give time to think about it. When Jordan goes for a drive, he removes himself from the situation at hand and gives himself time to ponder on what the right answer is for that situation. He wants to ensure that his response is one that is soaked in both prayer and thought. When Jordan returns from his drives, he normally has an answer, and his wife can rest in knowing that this time away was spent thinking and praying on the task at hand.

As Christians, we should pursue a similar line of thinking. This does not mean you need to go for a drive every time. But when issues arise, the wisest action one can take is the removal of oneself from a problem to think and pray on it. We do not have to have an answer at that precise moment. We do not have to have the perfect response to a problem, either. But we can always communicate that we care about the issue at hand if we give it a little thought. So, when situations arise, take time to think and pray.

HEAVENLY FATHER, REMIND ME TO THINK BEFORE I SPEAK. REMIND ME TO SEEK YOU IN THE MOMENTS WHEN I DO NOT KNOW WHAT TO DO. ALLOW ME TO HAVE TIME TO THINK AND COME TO YOU WHEN PROBLEMS ARISE BEFORE MAKING A DECISION. I WANT EVERY MOVE I MAKE TO BE SOMETHING I COME TO YOU IN CONSULTATION. ALLOW ME TO DO SO. AMEN.

97

PRAY ANYWHERE

Now as we have many parts in one body, and all
the parts do not have the same function, in the
same way we who are many are one body in Christ
and individually members of one another.

ROMANS 12:4–5

Many times, the best way to find peace is to go to God in prayer. Even though it is ideal for us to go to a secret place to commune with God, we must also remember the tremendous joy in knowing that God is always listening. There is never a time when we have to worry about Him not hearing us. If that is the case, should we not celebrate the fact that we can pray anywhere at any time? Should we not find peace in knowing that we can always approach God no matter the circumstance?

No one has learned this lesson better than Mary Jane. As a church elder's wife, she is familiar with prayer. She is a part of the women's ministry at the church. She takes part in her weekly prayer meeting at the church, and we should note that if there is a meal provided at the church, she has had something to do with it in the kitchen. Mary Jane is not only active in the work of the church, but she is also dedicated to it.

Something she has had to learn, however, is the informality of prayer. Informality does not mean that one gets to approach the Lord as anything less than the Creator of the universe, it just means that a person can pray to

197

Lord anywhere at any time. Though Mary Jane is active in her prayer life, she is very formal with it. She takes prayer seriously. So, whether she prays at home or church, she goes to her knees, plants her elbows, laces her fingers, and approaches the throne.

She will spend however long it takes to communicate with God, but she will only do so in a way that she thinks is respectful. So, it was odd for her to pick up a friend to take her to church. While on the way, they passed a man walking on the side of the road. They did not stop, but while Mary Jane drove, her friend closed her eyes and said, "Lord, please be with that man. Keep him safe."

Mary Jane planned to pray for the man once they arrived at church but watching her friend go to God while sitting in the front seat of a car was something she rarely did. If it was an immediate enough prayer, she would rather pull over and pray there than to just throw a prayer to heaven informally. When Mary Jane asked her friend about her decision to pray in the car and not at the church, she cheekily responded, "Mary Jane, the church is about the body, not the building."

LORD, I THANK YOU FOR BEING LORD OF ALL CREATION. REMIND ME THAT CHURCH IS NOT A BUILDING. IT IS A BODY OF BELIEVERS. REMIND ME THAT I CAN GO TO YOU WHEREVER I AM. AMEN.

LIVING BOLDLY

Paul stayed two whole years in his own rented house.
And he welcomed all who visited him, proclaiming
the kingdom of God and teaching about the Lord
Jesus Christ with all boldness and without hindrance.

ACTS 28:30–31

It seems strange to find an entry in a book about being still and finding peace that calls the reader to live boldly, but there is a reason it is in here. Living boldly does not necessarily mean that God called us to a sentiment of action, but it does mean living boldly in one's faith. In a world where so many of us have to wonder about the right words or the correct phrases, we must know that when it comes to our faith, there is a peace that comes from knowing that as long as we speak according to Scripture, we can rest knowing that what we are saying is favorable to God.

We all have one person in our lives who we believe has lived boldly for the faith. They know the Word. Bible verses season their words. Prayer is a weapon against the devil, and spreading the gospel comes first. There is an intensity to these people. And even though their personality may make us a little uncomfortable, the discomfort is often overshadowed by our respect for them. Why do we respect that which is uncomfortable? Why do we acknowledge there is a part of us that wishes we lived with the kind of boldness they carry? Well, it is probably because somewhere, deep down, we know this is how we are supposed to live.

We all have that person. This is the person who models for us how to live. We know that we have biblical figures who provide the same, but there is something special about witnessing someone who has taken biblical teaching and put it into practice. We admire those who apply what the Bible teaches.

One of the biggest reasons we respect these people is because even in their boldness they walk with a sense of confidence. They live in peace knowing that they are living the way God has called them to live. Boldness provides peace. Those who are boldly living out the faith have shifted their perspectives. They no longer worry about what they look like to the world. They do not care if they come off as weird or pushy or fanatical. They only care that they are doing what God has called them to do. They are not afraid to tell you the truth of Scripture, but just as the Bible calls us to spread the knowledge of God with love and grace, they make sure their boldness is seasoned with humility. When you live the way God has called you to live, the gift of peace in our soul is the reward.

HEAVENLY FATHER, I KNOW I HAVE MUCH TO LEARN. THANK YOU FOR SENDING ME PEOPLE WHO BOLDLY LIVE OUT THEIR FAITH. GIVE ME THE OPPORTUNITIES TO EXERCISE WHAT YOUR WORD SAYS AND ALLOW ME TO DO IT WITH BOLDNESS. AMEN.

THE ARMOR OF GOD

Put on the full armor of God so that you can stand against the schemes of the devil. For our struggle is not against flesh and blood, but against the rulers, against the authorities, against the cosmic powers of this darkness, against evil, spiritual forces in the heavens.

EPHESIANS 6:11–12

Body armor is something that mainly soldiers and police officers wear. Men and women of action are the ones who are tasked with having to put on such things. Then, why is it in a book about peace? Well, as the Bible tells us to put on the full armor of God, we must understand the relevance of such a statement regarding the peace it brings to the wearer. When a soldier puts on armor, they are not given peace over the war that is ahead of them—there is still a level of trepidation when approaching an upcoming battle—but there is a sense of peace in knowing they are somewhat protected.

As soldiers and law enforcers rally to take on a threat, they have to prepare. They gear up for the unknown. They make sure that whatever they may potentially need is on them. They wear pads that protect them from falls, bumps, or scrapes, and special fabric covers the bodies of officers and soldiers to keep shards from cutting flesh. They wear helmets and vests which protect vital organs from gunfire. There is a reason everything they wear falls under the umbrella of tactical gear. They plan for the worst. Training gives them the know-how on what to do in certain situations, but they also know that they are human.

They know that you cannot prepare for everything. Sometimes, you are going to need a little protection. It does not matter whether you are dealing with the elements or from threatening figures. The best thing you can do is have a little bit of protection for those moments.

As Christians, we must understand the phrase spiritual warfare. It is not only a metaphorical term. We can do everything in our power to prepare for upcoming temptations, but if we are not protected by the armor of God, we will all eventually fall. God knows we are unable to do this on our own. It is why we are warned about Christian warfare in Scripture. We must ready ourselves with truth, righteousness, peace, faith, salvation, and the Word of God.

God knew from the very beginning that we needed all of these for protection from evil. It does not mean that we can skip out on the battle. All of us will at one time have to take a stand in one form or the other. So, what would you rather have? An attempt to protect yourself or putting on the whole armor of God?

LORD, I KNOW THAT THERE IS A BATTLE GOING ON. I KNOW THAT SOULS HANG IN THE BALANCE, AND I AM THANKFUL THAT I AM ON THIS SIDE OF THE BATTLE. PROTECT ME, LORD. REMIND ME THAT I AM PROTECTED BY YOUR ARMOR. AMEN.

A GOOD PAIR
OF BOOTS

**But God proves his own love for us in that while
we were still sinners, Christ died for us.**

ROMANS 5:8

Maybe you have a blue-collar job or one that comes with a white-collar. You may find yourself to be an outdoors enthusiast, or you may be someone who enjoys air conditioning. Whatever the case may be, it always helps to have a pair of good boots. They need to be durable, comfortable, and able to withstand just about anything thrown at them. With a good pair of boots, a person feels ready. They feel as if the world beneath their feet is one that can be handled. They may even cost an amount of money you do not want to spend. But in the boot world, the price you pay communicates the quality.

This tendency is not always the case. For instance, many of us have had the opportunity to laugh at someone for spending fifty dollars on a T-shirt. How many of us have had to keep ourselves from rolling our eyes when someone spent half a thousand dollars on a pair of sneakers? In this country, a person can find ways to spend a large amount of money on things they do not need.

But regardless of how you feel about the boot industry, you cannot deny that they are built to last for years. The lifetime of most work boots that are over one hundred dollars typically is five years if they are worn regularly. Many workers will spend an extra twenty or thirty dollars for insoles to add a few more years of life to the boots. For factory workers, mechanics, lumberjacks, and outdoorsmen, quality is valuable. They would rather spend two hundred dollars on a good pair of boots that last five years than sixty dollars on a pair that they will have to replace every year. High quality is often associated with a high cost. So, to live with good quality, we are willing to make a larger sacrifice.

In the Christian world, we see this with Christ's sacrifice. Over the centuries, we have watched civilization after civilization make sacrifices to appease God. The problem is that this plan was never sustainable. Animal sacrifice was never going to be enough to atone for the sin of man. A higher cost was required, and even though it was a terrible cost, we can be still with thanksgiving in knowing that the sacrifice Christ made was sufficient for the eternal life of our souls.

No matter how much money we saved, no matter how much sin we avoided, there was never going to be a way for us to repay the debt that was accrued. Christ was the only one who could pay that debt. So, we can live in peace knowing that the eternal quality of our salvation could only come from the ultimate price Christ paid on the cross.

JESUS, THANK YOU FOR YOUR SACRIFICE ON THE CROSS. THANK YOU FOR MY SALVATION. THANK YOU FOR PAYING A PRICE I NEVER COULD. AMEN.

ROAD CLOSED

**A friend loves at all times, and a brother
is born for a difficult time.**

PROVERBS 17:17

When Brittany and five of her friends rented a cabin in Gatlinburg, she thought she had just booked the vacation of a lifetime. Off the back porch was a breathtaking view of the Smokey Mountains. It had five bedrooms, an open living room, a giant television. And when they arrived, the six young women filled the kitchen with enough snack foods to get them through their extended weekend together.

Each morning they would wake up, make breakfast together, and start the day by going into town to explore nature, shop in the outlet mall, catch lunch at a restaurant, and go to one of the silly attractions that made the tourist hot spot infamous. Then, when the sun started to set, the girls would pack in the cars, go back to the cabin, change into comfy clothes and watch movies and allow the snacks to be their dinner.

This four-day vacation, however, took a strange turn when the girls woke up on their third day. When Brittany plopped down on the couch, they raised the remote to turn on the television, but the remote would not work. She stood up and walked to the television, hit the power button, but it would not react. So, being the investigator, she walked to the light switch, flipped it on, and noticed the light would not react either. "I think the power is out." She said, assuming that something must be wrong with the cabin.

It did not matter that much to the girls. It was their last full day, and they assumed they would have breakfast in town. The girls piled up in the car, however, and discovered why their power was out. A tree had fallen on a power line and was now blocking the quickest way to town. The road in the other direction would take them two hours out of their way just to get to where they needed to go.

So, instead of going into town, the girls decided they would make the best of their situation. They built a fire. They got out some board games, and they ate their snacks. Then, around lunchtime, the lights came back on. The TV started making noise again. With all of the electronics turning on at once, they realized how loud their distracting world was. Brittany, seeing the quiet sadness from losing their time without distraction, stood up, unplugged the TV, and switched off the lights. She looked at her friends and said, "We can pretend for another hour or so."

LORD, I KNOW THERE ARE TIMES WHEN I HAVE ALLOWED DISTRACTION TO KEEP ME FROM SPENDING TIME WITH LOVED ONES. REMIND ME OF THE JOY THAT COMES FROM SPENDING TIME WITH LOVED ONES AND THANK YOU FOR PUTTING SUCH SPECIAL PEOPLE IN MY LIFE. ALLOW ME TO HAVE MOMENTS WITHOUT DISTRACTION WITH THE ONES I LOVE. AMEN.

MOM'S BLANKET

And we have come to know and to believe
the love that God has for us. God is love,
and the one who remains in love remains
in God, and God remains in him.

1 JOHN 4:16

Tiffany's daughter had a rule that she had come to live by. She was no longer content with her bedroom being as it was. She said that she could only fall asleep if Mom would lay with her and read her a story. Tiffany gladly took these opportunities, knowing that one day they would not be as available. So, she would come into the bedroom with her plush blanket, drape it over her daughter, and would read her a story from her favorite book. Tiffany's daughter would nestle herself deeper in the bed and listen to the voices her mother would use to bring life to the story. As her mother read to her, Tiffany's daughter's eyes would grow heavier and heavier until she eventually fell asleep.

As the months passed, Tiffany's daughter started to act like she was too old to be read to at night. She enjoyed her mother's company, of course, but being read to was for "little kids." So, her mother started only tucking her in and kissing her forehead before leaving the room.

After a few more months passed, Tiffany's daughter decided that a simple "Good night . . ." would do nicely. So, at her daughter's request, her mother would go into the room, tuck her in, and give a parting word before turning off the lights and leaving the room.

Finally, after a few more months of preparation, Tiffany's daughter announced that she would be going to bed alone. According to her logic, at the age of seven, she was now a big girl, and it was high time for her to start acting as such. So, she walked to her mother, kissed her on the cheek, and started leaving the room. As she rounded the corner, however, she looked to her mother and motioned for the blanket. Tiffany smirked and tossed it to her daughter and watched as she ran off to bed dragging the blanket behind her. Ten minutes passed. Then, her little girl appeared again, "I would like some help with my blanket, please."

Even at the age of seven, we can see glimpses of our desire for independence. We do not want to admit that we need help. If anything, we want to prove that we have it all together. But when the frustrations of the world come upon us, we begin to realize just how much we need help, even in the smallest of things. God gives us the security in knowing that He is with us. We can rest knowing that the Lord has gone before us. He has shown us the way through His Word. And like a child needing the security of a mother's blanket. God has covered our souls with an everlasting salvation.

FATHER, LIKE A CHILD, I HAVE TRIED TO LIVE INDEPENDENTLY FROM YOU. FORGIVE ME FOR THAT, LORD. YOU HAVE PROVEN YOUR LOVE FOR ME, AND I HAVE ACTED AS IF I DO NOT NEED IT. THANK YOU FOR LOVING ME AND COVERING ME WITH YOUR PROTECTION. AMEN.

103

GRANDMA'S PERFUME

I have treasured your word in my heart
so that I may not sin against you.

PSALM 119:11

Bethany is a girl of simple tastes. She decorates her home somewhat minimally. She dresses modestly, and even though she does well for herself, she is not one to flaunt her wealth. Bethany lives this way because of the example that was left by her grandparents. They were frugal people but knew the importance of paying for quality. They lived a good life, and because of their financial wisdom, they left behind a generous inheritance for their family.

Bethany took the inheritance money and put it in her retirement fund but made a request. Requests were outside of her normal behavior, so her family decided to listen. She asked if she could have her grandmother's perfume. The question seemed out of the ordinary. No one claimed it, nor did anyone seem to want it. But still, her parents wanted to know why she desired it. Bethany was never one to wear perfume.

"Well, I don't think I would ever wear it," she said, "but the smell reminds me of her. So, I thought that if ever start to miss her, I could always spray a bit and be reminded of her."

There was quiet in the room. No one knew what to say at the moment but understood the sentiment and granted the request. Years passed, and the memory of Bethany's grandmother faded. But now and again, she would spray a little bit of the perfume to be taken back to a happier time when her grandmother was alive. Even though she was happy that her grandmother was at peace and in the presence of the Father, she loved being reminded of the joy she shared when she spent time with her grandmother.

As Christians, we live with a similar sentiment. When we think about all that God has done for us and how He has loved us, it is only natural for us to have a longing to be with Him. This longing is, however, not something that should bring us sadness. It should provide us with excitement over that which is to come. We can look forward to the goodness that is to come from being in His presence.

So, if we are longing for our reunion with God, what is our perfume? What is our reminder of God's love? It is His Word. God grants us the privilege of knowing Him through the reading and studying of Scripture. We get to learn more and more about God, gaining a glimpse day by day of the Father who has loved us since before the beginning of time.

HEAVENLY FATHER, I AM SO THANKFUL I GET THE CHANCE TO GET TO KNOW YOU MORE. I AM SO GRATEFUL I HAVE THE OPPORTUNITY TO STUDY YOUR WORD AND LEARN MORE ABOUT YOU. INSTILL IN ME A HEART THAT DESIRES TO KNOW YOU MORE AND ALLOW ME THE TIME TO SPEND IN YOUR WORD. AMEN.

104

CHRISTMAS PAJAMAS

I have been crucified with Christ, and I no longer
live, but Christ lives in me. The life I now live
in the body, I live by faith in the Son of God,
who loved me and gave himself for me.

GALATIANS 2:20

Every Christmas, Connor's mother takes special care to get a gift for the family. Some years it has been as simple as going out to dinner at a nice restaurant. Other years, they have gone as far as to announce plans for a family vacation. This past year, Connor's mother decided to get the family matching pajamas.

Connor, admittedly, was a little annoyed at the gift. He had gotten everything that he had asked for, so he had assumed that this year's family gift was going to be just as extravagant. It is not that Connor was not thankful for the pajamas, but he just expected something different. Unbeknownst to him, something was different. He did not realize it until he put on his pajamas for the family picture.

Even though the exterior made them look like typical plaid pajamas, he realized that the inside was fleece. When he made the announcement, his sister remarked that hers were silk. His father's interior was wool. At this moment, Connor realized that even though the new nightwear was matching, the insides of these pajamas had been customized to the liking of the person wearing them. His sister loved all things silk, and other than the summer months, Connor's father always wore wool. Connor knew that even though they all received the same gift, they all had been uniquely loved in this gift.

The same can be said in the Christian faith. All Christians have received the gift of salvation, but each of us has a unique experience with God. Maybe you received the gift because you were raised in a Christian home where the Bible was discussed regularly. Perhaps you came to know the Lord after hitting rock bottom and turning to God. It could be that you fall somewhere in between the two. Whatever the case may be, even though the gift of salvation is the same for all of us, our experience is unique.

The point is that God distinctly knows you. You are known intricately. The gift of Christ's sacrifice covers all sins. But this is not necessarily a blanket statement. After all, there are certain sins you may never commit. But when the Bible says that Christ covered the sins of all those who would come to know Him, it means that God covered each individual's sins. He looked at your life and covered your sins personally just as He looked at mine and did the same. Our God loves each of us uniquely.

LORD, THANK YOU FOR LOVING ME. THANK YOU FOR THE GIFT OF SALVATION. I KNOW IT IS SOMETHING THAT I DO NOT DESERVE. PLEASE ALLOW ME TO LIVE CONFIDENTLY IN THE GIFT OF YOUR SACRIFICE AND KNOW IT WAS GIVEN PERSONALLY TO EACH OF YOUR CHILDREN. AMEN.

TRUSTING THE PROFESSIONALS

> "The LORD is the one who will go before you.
> He will be with you; he will not leave you or
> abandon you. Do not be afraid or discouraged."
>
> DEUTERONOMY 31:8

For Jonathan, it was difficult for him to admit that he needed the added motivation to get back in shape. In high school, he was a star athlete. There was not a week during school that he was not playing a sport of some kind. Now, he feels like he would be unrecognizable if any of his old teammates were to see him. He wanted to get back to where he was, or at least he wanted to look the part. So, he filled out an application to sign up for a 10-week commitment with a personal trainer.

The next week, he met his trainer. His coach was everything you would expect. He was energetic, passionate, looked like he could outrun a car and lift it over his head. But despite his energy, there was an understanding nature to him. He said, "I know you probably want to get in shape fast. We can do that in ten weeks, but I want you to know that I want you to get in shape the right way."

Jonathan understood that logic. He was not interested in only looking fit at the pool. Jonathan wanted to be healthy. So, he said that he would follow the guidance of the professional. That first day, the trainer had Jonathan go through a fitness test. He wanted to see how fast he could run a mile, and see how many pull-ups, push-ups, and air squats he could do in five minutes for each exercise. Jonathan ran a mile in twelve minutes and thirty-seven seconds. He was able to do eighty push-ups, twenty pull-ups, and one hundred and ten air squats in five minutes for each.

He was exhausted after the workout, and his coach told him to return the next day. For the first week, Jonathan felt insulted. His workout seemed to be too easy. He walked on the treadmill for forty-five minutes and only did light-weight exercises. Where were the grueling workouts of his former athleticism? Why was he doing minimal weight with a focus on form? He was a former athlete. Should he not be treated like one?

After two weeks of this treatment, Jonathan asked for a new coach, but when Jonathan saw his record, he noticed that his coach had a five-star rating and had nearly four hundred clients over the past ten years. His coach saw him looking at the roster and told him that everyone does not want him in the beginning, but if they trust the program, they are always happy with the results.

Still questioning his choice, he agreed to keep him as his coach. "Good," his coach said, "let's do your two-week check-in." Jonathan got on the treadmill and ran a mile as fast as he could. He ran it in ten minutes and twelve seconds. It was not fast, but it was faster. "If you trust me," his coach said, "you'll see the results you're after."

LORD, I KNOW I HAVE TO BE WILLING TO TRUST THE WISDOM OF THOSE YOU HAVE PUT BEFORE ME. ALLOW ME TO BE STILL AND HEED THEIR WORDS. AMEN.

106

POOL WITH DAD

*Our citizenship is in heaven, and we eagerly wait
for a Savior from there, the Lord Jesus Christ. He
will transform the body of our humble condition
into the likeness of his glorious body, by the power
that enables him to subject everything to himself.*

PHILIPPIANS 3:20–21

Jerry was not an extravagant man. He had driven the same car for many years. He only bought refurbished phones, and unless the occasion demanded it, Jerry wore clothes that you could find at a local big-box store. There was, however, one place where he liked to spend his money. Jerry enjoyed playing pool. So, even though his home looked modest in most areas, he had a room that he had turned into a billiard room.

In his little pool hall, he had a television mounted on the wall so that he could watch the news or whatever game was on. He had leather chairs that were off to the side so that he would sit and read, watch television, or sink into them and fall asleep. It was his retirement gift to himself. He wanted to be good enough to compete at tournaments. He even started getting his sons involved so that they could have a bonding time whenever they were in town. It was a way to cut loose. It was a mechanism they could use to discuss politics and religion. And above all, it was a competitive skill that he could use to keep up with his sons.

As he grew older, his skills started to fade. He could not hold the pool stick as steady as he once did. He could not gauge certain angles the way he once could, and his back would not allow him to stretch over the table the way he once did. His billiard room only served as a reminder that he was getting older and that his time on this earth was coming to a close.

In his last month of life, Jerry asked his adult sons to teach their children how to play and allow him to watch. They guided their father into the billiard room, sat him in his chair, and played games for a few hours with their kids. There was laughter over silly mistakes, celebration over seemingly impossible shots, and playful banter to try and trip up focus. It was a moment that all of them wished to live in forever.

In his last moment, he asked that his sons promise to play each other for who would receive ownership of the table. The day after the funeral. The boys played, wishing they could play with their father, but loving the fact that their father who loved the Lord more than he loved pool was probably playing pool now with a new body if such a game is even played in heaven.

LORD, AS WE GET OLDER, WE CAN REST IN THE KNOWLEDGE THAT THERE IS A PLACE WHERE WE WILL RUN AND NOT GROW WEARY. THANK YOU FOR THE GIFT OF ETERNAL LIFE AND THANK YOU FOR SHOWING US A LOVE THAT SPANS INTO ETERNITY. AMEN.

107

BIG CHURCH

**Now to him who is able to do above and
beyond all that we ask or think according
to the power that works in us—to him be
glory in the church and in Christ Jesus to all
generations, forever and ever. Amen.**

EPHESIANS 3:20–21

Blake had always dreamed of going to "Big Church." His church had a children's church program that went from three-year-old all the way to second grade. During his second-grade year, coloring pictures of Jesus and singing songs about how much He loved us were beginning to lose their appeal. Not only that, but his older brother was able to attend Big Church. He wanted to be with his older sibling, and the children's church was one of the many things that hindered him from being with his brother.

When he graduated from the second grade, he walked confidently past the hallway where you drop the "little kids" off and followed his family into the sanctuary. To say that he was shocked was an understatement. He did not know what he expected, but it was not this. Where were the coloring books? He assumed he would not use crayons anymore, but how could he color without coloring pencils? Not only that, but where were the coloring sheets? He knew they would not be the hokey drawings of a cartoon lion and lamb sleeping next to each other, but he expected to color something. And finally, what was with these songs? They did not have a catchy verse, and they had to be sung from a book that he could barely read.

And yet, he looked up to his teenage brother, who sang the songs confidently and with joy. Blake knew that there must be something that he was missing. He did not yet know what. With each week, he mimicked his brother. He stood the way he stood. He sang the way he sang and leaned forward in his seat the same way his brother did. Although it had not dawned on Blake yet, he began copying the way he dressed and the way he wore his hair. If his brother wore brown socks, then he would wear brown socks. He was dedicated to looking just like his brother.

After two months of going to Big Church, he finally asked his brother why he liked church as much as he did. After a moment of thought, his brother said, "Well, I know our church is boring sometimes. I know the songs seem a little old, but when you know you are going to church to worship God, you do not care about what is going on in the church as long as it is bringing glory to Him."

Blake, still not understanding, asked how to bring glory to God. His brother said, "I guess you learn more about Him the more you get to know Him."

Blake paused and asked, "Well, how do I know God and how do I bring Him glory?"

LORD, I WANT TO KNOW YOU. I WANT TO BRING GLORY TO YOU. SHOW ME HOW TO BRING YOU GLORY. ALLOW ME TO DISCOVER A POSTURE THAT POINTS OTHERS TO YOU. AMEN.

REVERENCE IN PRAYER

For this reason God highly exalted him and gave him the name that is above every name, so that at the name of Jesus every knee will bow—in heaven and on earth and under the earth—and every tongue will confess that Jesus Christ is Lord, to the glory of God the Father.

PHILIPPIANS 2:9–11

One thing that many have noticed about churches no matter the denomination is the reverence of believers during moments of prayer. Whether your church is more focused on its charisma and style or its liturgy and doctrine, there is a striking similarity between culturally different churches. This similarity is found in their attitude during prayer.

Some may have their hands in the air while others have them gripping the pew. Some may have whispers under their breath while others pray in complete silence. Whatever congregation you find yourself in, you will notice the humility of those who treat God as who He is: the all-powerful, all-knowing, and all-loving Creator. Are there some churches that veer away from this attitude? Yes, of course. Some make the mistake of only talking to God from the perspective of a "bro" with whom you get to talk and hang out. This attitude is irreverent and misses the identity of who God is. But by in large, most biblically centered churches understand the majesty and lordship of God and treat Him with the appropriate level of respect.

When we go to God in reverence, we are acknowledging the reality of who God is. When we do this, we receive a sense of peace in knowing the identity of the God to whom we are speaking. We are not talking to some guy who has ultimate power and we can "totally chill with." We are coming before the Lord of all creation. The being who represents the first cause. The God with perfect foreknowledge. The God who knows the hairs on your head, who knit you in the womb, who knew your call before you knew your name. That is the kind of being we are discussing.

So, when we stand before God and pray to Him with reverence, our only response should be a still spirit and a willingness to act according to His will. Anything less than that is not only disrespectful but a guarantee of potential fear for the all-powerful Creator of the universe. So, pray to God. Lean on Him. Know that He is not only loving, but his identity is love itself. The respect of God should be nothing less than the ultimate level of respect you can have. Whether your hands are in the air and your eyes are open or your head is bowed and your eyes are closed, what does posture show? Are you humbly standing before God, or are you treating Him as your equal?

LORD, I KNOW THERE HAVE BEEN MOMENTS WHEN I HAVE TREATED YOU AS LESS THAN YOU ARE. I ASK FOR YOUR FORGIVENESS IN THOSE MOMENTS. LORD, I COME TO YOU TODAY IN REVERENCE AND ASK THAT YOU CHANGE MY HEART AND LEAD ME TO THE POSTURE I SHOULD HAVE IN YOUR PRESENCE. I WANT TO BE OBEDIENT, LORD. HELP ME IN THIS WAY. AMEN.

109

MAKE MARK SMIRK

"When an alien resides with you in your land, you
must not oppress him. You will regard the alien
who resides with you as the native-born among you.
You are to love him as yourself, for you were aliens
in the land of Egypt; I am the LORD your God."

LEVITICUS 19:33–34

Mark is a man of seriousness. He rarely laughs and is not one to share a joke at the watercooler. This does not mean that he is not kind or lacks approachability, but when he is at work, he is there to work. It is as simple as that. There is, however, a game played at the office: "Make Mark Smirk." The rules of the game are simple, but few have won. There is only one rule; as long as the joke does not interfere with work, and is appropriate, anything goes. The office has started to take this competition seriously. There is even a whiteboard that keeps up with the score for the year. Last year, the one who had made Mark smirk the most walked home with a twenty-dollar gift card. Mark received one as well for being a good sport.

When a new team leader joined the team, she was quick to notice the game and was not a fan. She felt horrible for Mark and thought that they must be making fun of him. She observed for a few weeks before she decided on the morality of playing such a game. Before she decided to file a complaint, she approached Mark and asked him why he allowed them to play pranks on them. He deserved to be respected.

Mark, knowing that she was new to the team, pointed to the small whiteboard on one of his teammate's desk. He said, "This is a game that I agreed to play and was told that if I ever get tired of it, just to let them know. I am an accountant. I play with numbers all day. And even though I am good at my job, it can be very monotonous from time to time. So, when this game was proposed, I was all for it." When she pushed him on why he should not be, Mark explained further. "When I lead meetings, I am treated with the utmost respect. They care about what I have to say. They seek my wisdom on topics outside of work. They respect me."

With one final attempt to dissuade him, he provided a little more honesty as to why he allows the game to be played, "I am a long way from home, but just as I am serious here, I am serious with my family. They do the same thing. Now, the team does not know this, but the day they invented this game was one of the happiest days in this company because whether they know it or not, they treat me like family."

The new team leader softened at this news. She said, "I will allow it then, and if playing it makes you feel like family, I hope to get on the board soon." At this, she made Mark smirk and earned a spot on the board with the rest of the team.

LORD, I HOPE TO TREAT OTHERS LIKE FAMILY. REMIND ME TO BRING PEACE TO OTHERS BY TREATING THEM LIKE MY LOVED ONES. AMEN.

110

NOTHING'S WRONG!

But he said to me, "My grace is sufficient for you, for my power is perfected in weakness." Therefore, I will most gladly boast all the more about my weaknesses, so that Christ's power may reside in me.

2 CORINTHIANS 12:9

As we have already discussed, there is nothing wrong with seriousness or humor in the workplace. People who take their job seriously and have fun doing it are often the most sought-after candidates. But when a person clings to solemnity, there is often the danger of building a wall around oneself, protecting themselves from showing any vulnerability. A person cannot live like this long.

One's vulnerability can be a good thing to share. Oversharing can become a problem, but those we love would rather have us be honest with them than charge ahead with an over-serious attitude or a silly one that pulls their attention away from their problems.

No one has learned this lesson quite like Craig. Craig is the funny one in the office as well as one of the top performers. He always meets his numbers. Craig comes in under budget and is one of the team favorites when it comes down to helping out other teammates when they are in need. He has never asked for help, nor has he ever showed any sign of needing help. Now, this could not be further from the truth.

Craig arrives at work hours earlier than anyone else and leaves hours after the last person does. He stays up late to do work that is starting to pile up. Now, because of his efforts, the company has been able to grow in many areas. And because it appears that he has such a handle on everything, few have asked him if he needs help with anything. And when they do ask, he always says something along the lines that he will need help one day, but he has a good handle on it. Working thirteen-hour days in secret is not the definition of having a good handle on it.

One afternoon, Craig was called into his manager's office. He was not sure what this was about. He had met all of his deadlines and was about to take on a new project. When he sat down, he had four résumés set in front of him. His manager spoke frankly, but lovingly, "I'm not going to mince words with you, Craig. We've watched the cameras for the past two weeks. You're killing yourself. I'm not going to lose my top performer because he refuses to admit that he needs help. You are going to help me find you an assistant."

Tears welled in his eyes, and he made a promise that he had his job under control but was told firmly again, "Craig, you don't, and it is not because you're not great at your job, it is because you are refusing to ask for help."

HEAVENLY FATHER, PLEASE ALLOW ME TO BE VULNERABLE. REMIND ME TO BE HONEST WITH MYSELF AND OTHERS, AND ALLOW ME TO HAVE MOMENTS OF VULNERABILITY WITH THOSE I CARE ABOUT. AMEN.

111

TRUST IN HIM

Now if any of you lacks wisdom, he should ask God—who gives to all generously and ungrudgingly—and it will be given to him.

JAMES 1:5

We all know that we are supposed to place our trust in God. Trust in God seems like simple information, but just because something is simple does not mean that it is easy. After all, climbing a mountain is pretty straightforward. All one has to do is put one foot in front of the other. And yet, it is one of the most challenging sports to undertake.

To put one's trust in God is to communicate that in all circumstances, you will choose to rest in Him. Your spiritual harmony does not come from your surroundings. It comes from the supplier of perfect peace. So why does it sound so easy while at the same time remarkably difficult? Well, it is because we have come to understand that nothing about this life is easy. When the bills come in and we do not have enough money in our bank account to cover the cost, is it still that easy? When our child needs school supplies, but all we can do is choose between peanut butter and markers, is it still that easy? The answer, of course, is no. It is not always easy to place our trust in God. There is a reason we are warned that our faith will be tested.

Maybe the problem is not always financial. What if you are dealing with health issues that cause you to lean on the Lord for understanding? Is it still easy, then? Does it get easier? How do we have faith when our circumstances are so frustrating?

It should be said that some of Paul's most hopeful writings came from a prison cell. He was someone who would have been in danger of execution. He was preaching the gospel in a land that was hostile toward its message. And yet, he speaks of the possibilities with God. He displays a fearlessness in the most fearful of predicaments. Was it easy for Paul to do this? Of course, not! Any look at his circumstances would break the strongest of men. And yet, Paul viewed the potential of his frustrations with joy. He spoke with power and excitement because he knew where his trust was. It was not in ways of the world, nor was it found in blind hope for the future. Paul had his eyes on the Kingdom of God. He kept his vision on bringing glory to God.

To place one's trust in God is to do something intentionally. It is to communicate with all parties involved that your faith is not in this world but to stand firm on the promises of God and trust in them.

LORD, REMIND ME TO PUT MY TRUST IN YOU. REMIND ME TO LEAN NOT ON MY UNDERSTANDING, BUT TO STAND IN UNSHAKABLE FAITH IN THE PROMISES YOU HAVE OVER MY FUTURE. THANK YOU, LORD, FOR ALL THAT YOU DO AND PROVE TO DO THROUGH YOUR WORD. AMEN.

112

BREAKFAST BURRITOS AND THE BIBLE

*The people here were of more noble character
than those in Thessalonica, since they received
the word with eagerness and examined the
Scriptures daily to see if these things were so.*

ACTS 17:11

Many church members have at least heard of a community group or life group, but in every church across the nation, there is a building trend toward the development of discipleship groups. What is the difference? Well, the secret is found in the names. A community group, or life group, is a group based around the notion of creating community with each other. A discipleship group is about being sharpened through scriptural study. Community groups offer biblical study, but their intention is more on the focus of building fellowship. With discipleship groups, fellowship is built naturally within the group, but the group intends to study the Word of God.

For Jake, it is one of his favorite days of the week. On one hand, he gets to spend time with a group of guys that he has come to love and admire while they study the Bible together. And on the other hand, he gets to cheat a little bit on his diet and enjoy a breakfast burrito at their local diner. The same thing happens every Saturday morning. Jake wakes up around six, does his morning routine, throws on some clothes that he does not care about, and arrives at the diner around seven. The men sit down, order food, drink coffee, and catch up with each other on what all has happened to them throughout the week. Then, after thirty minutes of catching up and filling bellies, the men begin to dive into the Word.

In Jake's group, he sits with a Sunday school teacher, an associate pastor, and a seminary graduate. He would be a liar if he told you that he was not intimidated by the group, but he's good friends with all of them, and they asked him to join the group.

What Jake gleaned from the study was that even though these men all knew the Bible, they never stopped studying it the way they all were originally taught. He, at first, was worried that there was going to be an overuse of jargon. And even though there were times when it appeared, it was never so over the top that he could not keep up. The four of them went through Scripture verse by verse and broke it down word by word. For the first time, he felt like biblical study was going at his pace. They did not jump ahead to another part of the Bible. They stayed in that specific verse and discussed what their study Bibles had to say about it. By doing this, he learned how to use his study Bible. The Word of God gained color, and he was able to see more of the context of Scripture, all of this while enjoying good coffee, food, and fellowship.

LORD, REMIND ME OF THE GOODNESS THAT COMES FROM STUDYING YOUR WORD WITH OTHER BELIEVERS. ALLOW ME TO FIND PEOPLE TO SHARPEN ME AND PROVIDE ME OPPORTUNITIES THAT WILL ALLOW ME TO GAIN MORE KNOWLEDGE OF YOU AND YOUR WORD. AMEN.

MOMMA, LOOK!

"Whenever you pray, you must not be like the
hypocrites, because they love to pray standing in the
synagogues and on the street corners to be seen by
people. Truly I tell you, they have their reward."

MATTHEW 6:5

If you have children, you have more than likely heard this phrase. There is a desire from an early age to be known. Parents from every generation have had to deal with our focus being pulled away from work, entertainment, or responsibilities to spend time giving our children undivided attention. Even though we sometimes scold our children for being selfish with time that does not belong to them, this is a feeling that does not ever go away. We, as children of God, still seek attention from the Father.

We want to make God proud, as any child wants to make their parent proud, but we need to think about our intentions behind our actions when we seek God's attention. Think of a child for a second. It can be your child, a niece or a nephew, or maybe even a child that you take care of from time to time. Think why they ask for your attention when they do. Is it because they want to please you or because they want you to look at how impressive they are?

For example, two children could pick flowers for their grandmother. When they come to her, one says, "Grandma, I picked you flowers." But the other may say, "But I picked more!" Which of these is rooted in service and which of these is rooted in selfishness? If we take the time to look at the two, it is easy to see which child cares about their grandmother and which one cares about being seen by their grandmother. One is selfless and the other is selfish.

In Christian service, we need to be careful not to fall into the same trap. Do we spend time with God in private with quiet humble hearts or do we do it in public for others to hear eloquent speeches pointed at God? Both are prayers, but which one comes from selfless action and which one comes from boisterous behavior?

Of course, God wants us to seek Him. His very nature is to know and be known. But we must also check our hearts before we stand before the Lord. Is our heart selfless or is our heart selfish? Are we coming to God to check a box, or are we coming to Him to commune with the Father? Our goal should not be to seek God to show how impressive we are because we remembered to pray with Him every day. Our goal should be to spend time with Him because He is God. So, when you seek God, go to Him in humility. Know that He wants to hear You, but know that He also deserves to be approached with humility and love.

HEAVENLY FATHER, I KNOW THAT I HAVE COME BEFORE YOU TO ONLY GET YOUR ATTENTION OVER MY NEEDS. I HAVE TRIED TO MANIPULATE YOU BY SHOWING HOW DEVOUT I AM. FORGIVE ME FOR THIS, LORD. REMIND ME TO COME TO YOU IN HUMILITY. AMEN.

"I'LL ALWAYS BE WITH YOU"

"Go, therefore, and make disciples of all nations,
baptizing them in the name of the Father and of the
Son and of the Holy Spirit, teaching them to observe
everything I have commanded you. And remember,
I am with you always, to the end of the age."

MATTHEW 28:19–20

When Jason's grandmother was dying, to console him, she made a promise. She said that no matter what, she would always be with him. Theologically speaking, it is difficult to discuss the truth of such a statement, but we can recognize the sentiment. When she spoke, Jason's grandmother communicated that the memory of her would always be with him. It was a sad reality, but a reality that he could endure. The disciples, if we take a look at what the Bible says, probably felt a similar emotion when Jesus ascended into heaven.

These men, while standing with the physical Jesus, would have naturally felt a longing to go with Christ. Jesus, however, had already promised that His exit was temporary. He said that He was going to prepare a place for them and would return for them at the appointed time. What is incredible about this is that even with Jesus ascending into heaven, God gave the followers of His Son access to the Holy Spirit. God never left us. Even in the moments where they would have felt a longing to go with Christ, God revealed to the disciples the importance of spreading the gospel.

When Jason's grandmother passed away, he knew that she died loving the Lord. There was no question about that. The woman praised God's name in the margins of her Bible. And though there was sadness over the loss of her earthly life, Jason could live in peace and celebration. He knew that even though her body lay in front of him, she was long gone and standing before the Father. She was no longer weak. She was no longer tired. She was dancing at the feet of Jesus.

This earthly life will end. It has to end, but the joy of knowing Christ is the peace of mind in knowing what happens after earthly death. We go to heaven. Joy and peace are not found in our location. That is a shallow understanding of the gospel message. If all we have to look forward to after death is a location adjustment, then the joy of heaven would be temporary. No, the truest peace that comes from knowing God is the joy that comes from glorifying God for all eternity.

HEAVENLY FATHER, THANK YOU FOR SENDING YOUR SON TO DIE ON THE CROSS. I AM IN AWE OF THE GOODNESS YOU HAVE SHOWN BY ALLOWING HIM TO MAKE THE ULTIMATE SACRIFICE FOR MY SINS. LORD, REMIND ME DAILY OF THE GOODNESS OF THE GOSPEL. REMIND ME THAT I AM CHARGED WITH THE SAME RESPONSIBILITY TO SPREAD THE GOSPEL AND MAKE YOU KNOWN. THANK YOU, LORD, FOR BEING WITH ME ALWAYS. AMEN.

BRING ME NEAR

*But as for me, God's presence is my good.
I have made the Lord GOD my refuge,
so I can tell about all you do.*

PSALM 73:28

Depending on your church experience, it is likely you have heard this phrase in prayer. A pastor will call upon the Lord to "bring him near" to God. He is not speaking about literal proximity. But instead, he is giving a focus to the notion of recognizing being in God's presence. It may sound similar, but the implications are very different. To call on God to bring you near to Him is to claim that you want to be of a similar mind as Him. You want your will to be His will. You are asking God to align you to His desires and not your own.

It is a phrase that has become trite over the years. We have heard it stated from the pulpit so many times that it has almost lost its ability to affect the listener. It is one of those phrases that we may understand the gist but cannot define well. Because of this, we find ourselves in dangerous territory. We ask God to do something that we do not fully understand. To ask God to draw you near to Him is saying that you no longer want to be seen. You desire to be so close to God that they no longer see you; others only see a reflection of God.

This sentiment, though good to ask, comes with a tremendous price on one's life. You are willing to deny yourself. Can you do that? Do you have the courage to come up after Christ and live a Christ-like life? Few can. Many wish to be drawn near to the Lord. Many desire to live a life that reflects Christ, but few ever will because the life-change is too drastic. To follow Christ is to find suffering, to discover meekness, to live in humility. These descriptors are not appealing to the world. And as people born in this world, we have a natural inclination to wish to live a worldly life.

It is not an easy task to follow Christ, but there is peace in knowing you are on the right path. There will be moments where you fall. There will be times when you are tired, but the joy of following Christ comes from knowing you are heading in the right direction. So, do not get me wrong. I want you to ask God to draw you near. There is a peace beyond understanding, and God will provide a way to bring Him glory.

LORD, I AM PRAYING A RISKY PRAYER. I WANT YOU TO BRING ME NEAR TO YOU. I WANT MY WILL TO BE YOUR WILL. I WANT MY LIFE TO REFLECT YOU. DRAW ME NEAR TO YOU, LORD, AND GIVE ME THE COURAGE AND DRIVE TO POINT OTHERS TO YOU. ALLOW ME TO BE IN YOUR PRESENCE. AMEN.

116

"CAN YOU HEAR ME?"

When I was a child, I spoke like a child, I thought like a child, I reasoned like a child. When I became a man, I put aside childish things.

1 CORINTHIANS 13:11

There is nothing worse than not being able to connect with others. When you are driving through the countryside, you may benefit from the scenic views and the lack of traffic, but you are also cursed with being unable to reach people that you may need at that moment because of poor cell service. This specifically happens to Lisa every time she drives to church. On her drive, the fastest way to get to her church is by traveling down a street that splits two large farms. Nothing but wheat and corn fill the horizon. And even though this part of her drive only lasts for ten minutes, she is often filled with apprehension over the notion of not being able to speak to someone.

There are times that she has even tried to test this by making calls while on the road and seeing if she can hear what the other person is saying. The calls are spotty and often leave her yelling, "Can you hear me?!" You see, Lisa has a fear of being stranded. Even though she knows that she would be fine, she does not like the idea of something happening to her car and her not being able to get in contact with anyone. It is a sentiment that many who live in rural areas can understand.

What is interesting about this situation is that there are Christians who deal with a similar situation when they feel like they are far away from God. They know that the Lord is always with them. They understand that God will never leave them. Nevertheless, all Christians at one time or another have felt as if they are nowhere near God. Why does this feeling occur? How do Christians ever get into this mind-set?

The answer to this question is often found in the lifestyle of the Christians feeling this aloneness. Many of them will say that they are feeling far from God and will, at the same time, not be able to recall the last time they opened their Bible. Some will point to this feeling of abandonment and will also live a sinful lifestyle. Whatever the case may be, many will long to be with the Father and not be willing to put aside the foolishness of childish behavior.

This is not something to be taken lightly. A longing to be near God is a good thing, but a longing to be near God and an unwillingness to move closer to Him is a very dangerous thing. Come to God. Be with Him again and know the peace that comes from putting away childish things.

LORD, I KNOW I AM WRESTLING WITH THINGS THAT I SHOULD HAVE PUT AWAY A LONG TIME AGO. PLEASE GIVE ME A HEART THAT NO LONGER WANTS TO HAVE SUCH CHILDISH THINGS AS SIN. TURN MY HEART AWAY FROM SIN AND DRAW ME NEAR TO YOU. AMEN.

117

THIS IS MY SOLEMN VOW

Wives, submit to your husbands as to the Lord,
because the husband is the head of the wife as Christ
is the head of the church. He is the Savior of the
body. Now as the church submits to Christ, so also
wives are to submit to their husbands in everything.
Husbands, love your wives, just as Christ loved the
church and gave himself for her to make her holy,
cleansing her with the washing of water by the word.

EPHESIANS 5:22–26

Some weddings have started implementing "vow" language in their ceremonies. They will say their vows, and then after finishing, they will say, "This is my solemn vow." This addition is important for two reasons. For one reason, it communicates to God the seriousness of your statement. It is a reminder to the speaker that you are not just making a vow to your spouse. You are making that vow to God. So many young men and women approach the front of the church and say things flippantly with charged emotional language. They season emotion with Christianity when they should be focusing on their Christian duty to love and support one's spouse. For the other reason, it can be a provider of added peace to your partner, by communicating that you are making something more than a promise when you say you will spend the rest of your life with him or her.

This conversation brings up a bigger question. What is a vow? A vow, in its simplest definition, is a promise. To make a marriage vow is to promise to spend the rest of your life with your spouse, but it also serves as a promise to God that you will stand by the covenant of marriage. Your vow to God is to glorify Him through your marriage, nothing less.

When a marriage is ordained by God, the marriage's ordination is a communication to God, the couple, and the witnesses of the wedding ceremony, that this marriage will do the will of God. The husband vows to stand by his wife, to cherish her, to lead her well, to love her as Christ loved the church. The wife vows to support her husband, to submit to his leadership, and love him in sickness and in health.

The marriage vows were never meant to be taken lightly, and yet, so many people do. They become fickle. A partner does not act according to God's will, and it destroys the marriage in the process. The peace of a good marriage is discovered when it points others to God. Our role as married Christians is not only to love our spouse, though that is important and necessary, it is to glorify God.

So, if you are married, discover the peace in loving God with your spouse. Bring glory to God's Kingdom with your spouse, and point others to Christ.

HEAVENLY FATHER, I THANK YOU FOR THE GIFT OF MARRIAGE. I PRAY THAT YOU ALLOW ME THE CHANCE TO POINT OTHERS TO CHRIST THROUGH MY MARRIAGE. REMIND ME TO GLORIFY YOU WITH MY MARRIAGE AS I SHOULD IN MY LIFE. AMEN.

118

PLEASE FOLLOW THE INSTRUCTIONS

But grow in the grace and knowledge of our Lord and Savior Jesus Christ. To him be the glory both now and to the day of eternity.

2 PETER 3:18

Stephanie's husband is an engineer. He works primarily with medical supplies and helps create new ways of handling prosthetics. He writes out long manuals that teach other engineers and builders how to create the products according to his specifications. Because of his job, he claims that he has become a great appreciator of following the manual.

Stephanie, however, knows her husband well. She knows that even though he is a man who writes instructions for a living, he rarely follows them for things he assumes he can figure out on his own. This was not more evident than when they tried to put together a desk.

When they first saw the desk, it seemed like a natural thing to pursue. He did work that was both on a sketch pad and a computer screen. He needed a desk that would allow him to draw out plans and configurations, but he also needed one that would provide him plenty of room for a dual monitor and a keyboard. An L-shaped desk was the only option, and Stephanie was excited for her husband to have a place to work that was not spread out over the kitchen table.

When the box arrived, the two of them moved it to the bonus room to the corner where he would set up his home office. When they finally made the time to unbox everything and get to work, the first thing Stephanie's husband did was toss the directions on the couch and start sprawling out all of the pieces on the floor. He stood in front of all of it for a few moments, piecing it together in his mind. Stephanie knew where this was going. She watched as her husband sat on the ground and started jig-sawing a desk together with no help from the instructions.

While he got to work on it, she simply sat down and started reading the directions. After an hour of putting things together and seeing how they looked, he started getting frustrated. Stephanie asked if he wanted the instructions, but her husband was determined to do this by himself. Finally, after three hours of getting nowhere, he relented and asked for the manual.

It is amazing how similar this behavior is in the Christian world. Christians will try to figure out all of life's situations without consulting God. They may go to Him in prayer and will ask for wisdom but are rarely willing to go to His Word to seek that wisdom. Just as there is a benefit to using instructions to build a desk, there are benefits of peace that come with being a Christian who knows the Word.

LORD, ALLOW ME TO SPEND MORE TIME IN
YOUR WORD. REMIND ME TO TAKE YOUR
WORD SERIOUSLY AND APPLY IT TO MY LIFE.
REMIND ME OF YOUR GOODNESS, LORD,
AND ALLOW ME TO DISCOVER MORE OF IT
WHILE DIVING INTO SCRIPTURE. AMEN.

119

NEWSPAPER ROUTES

He was diligent in every deed that he began in the service of God's temple, in the instruction and the commands, in order to seek his God, and he prospered.

2 CHRONICLES 31:21

There are many "first jobs" that no longer exist the way they once did. There were times that before one turned sixteen, there were still ample opportunities to make a little bit of money before one could get a job at the proper age. You would find thirteen-year-olds working on farms. You might see a few preteens mowing yards for extra cash, but the select few could be entrusted in small towns all across America with a newspaper route.

Kids all over America could show up at a news press, collect as many papers as they could carry, get on their bikes, and toss them on porches, at front doors, in mailboxes, and on driveways throughout various neighborhoods all across the town. They would then return to collect more papers or would return to collect their pay for running their route. Because newsprint has, more or less, started to fade from society, so have newspaper routes, which is a shame.

It's a shame for a couple of reasons. For one, preteens lose a way to make more money to save for a car, or future dates, or even college, but there is an even greater reason why the disappearance of these job opportunities is such sad news. The fact is that these jobs taught lessons that seem to have almost fallen through the cracks in our society. They showed the importance of being prepared. They taught why it is so important to not allow the day to slip away from you. Newspaper routes, above all else, taught the joy that comes from a hard day's work at a young age.

Many people don't discover that joy until they are well into college. They may have snapshots of that kind of joy in school when they accomplish large projects or are a part of a team that has trained hard, but there is nothing quite like a day of hard work and the enjoyment of the benefits of that work. So, how do we teach those lessons today? How do relive the joy of hard work?

Well, the first thing we can do is look at work as a joy and not a burden. Being able to work holds the very acknowledgment of the gifts and abilities God has given each one of us. A long day's work is a joy because it most notably was spent using the gifts God has given you. The same way God blesses children with energy and endurance to ride bikes through town and deliver papers, God has given you special talents to get through the day and take joy in knowing that the day was spent using those talents.

LORD, THANK YOU FOR WORK. I KNOW THAT SOMETIMES I LOOK AT WORK AS IF IT IS SOME KIND OF BURDEN. ALLOW ME TO RECOGNIZE MY GIFTS AND USE THOSE GIFTS EACH DAY IN THE WORK YOU HAVE GIVEN ME. AMEN.

120

REMEMBER TO BE STILL

"For which of you, wanting to build a tower, doesn't first sit down and calculate the cost to see if he has enough to complete it? Otherwise, after he has laid the foundation and cannot finish it, all the onlookers will begin to ridicule him, saying, 'This man started to build and wasn't able to finish.'"

LUKE 14:28–30

You made it to the last devotional. You read stories, reminders, and concepts that all point to the importance of stillness. So, where do we go from here? Is this only going to be another book that was on the coffee table or nightstand? Will it be a book with a pretty cover that works as an eye-catching decoration? I hope this book has worked as a reminder of that which is ongoing.

As a pastor once said, the years of this life fly, but the days crawl. There were days that you probably did not feel like reading this. There may have been days that you skipped. Maybe this 120-day devotional turned into a 200-day journey. It does not matter. The fact is that if you have taken the time to treasure these scriptural truths, you have, hopefully, picked up a few tricks that will allow you to find a bit of silence in the day.

This last entry is a reminder to do something that you probably have long known by now. Please, do not be afraid to be still. I know there are times when it may seem foolish to do so. After all, there are so many things that need to be done. But trust me, there is a joy that comes with stillness. We all recognize that peace is an obvious enjoyment of stillness, but even though it may seem silent, joy is still joy.

So, when you go back into the world and all the distractions are back at the forefront, what are you going to do? You have to deal with them. They cannot be ignored, but when the difficulties come and the frustrations arrive, stop. Take a breath and go to God in prayer. Seek stillness in His presence and know that He is Lord of all.

When you feel like you cannot keep up with the kids, or there is just too much on your plate at work, who are you going to turn to? Life is going to be hard. It is a promise that a broken world gives, but when frustrations build in the early morning, turn to the one who created the sun. When difficulties come that can stir up strife, turn to the one whose identity is peace.

HEAVENLY FATHER, I KNOW THERE ARE GOING TO BE DAYS WHERE THE FRUSTRATIONS COME. I KNOW THERE ARE GOING TO BE MOMENTS WHEN I CANNOT FIND PEACE ON MY OWN. LORD, I PRAY IN THOSE MOMENTS THAT YOU PULL ME CLOSE TO YOU. REMIND ME TO LEAN ON YOU IN TIMES OF DIFFICULTY. REMIND ME THAT WHEN THE WORLD BRINGS ME CHAOS, IT IS YOU WHO BRINGS ME PEACE. AMEN.